VISIBILITY
4

DANNELLA BURNETT

Published by
Hybrid Global Publishing
333 E 14th Street
#3C
New York, NY 10003

Copyright © 2024 by Dannella Burnett

All rights reserved. No part of this book may be reproduced or transmitted in any form or by any means, electronic or mechanical, including photocopying, recording, or by any information storage and retrieval system, without the written permission of the Publisher, except where permitted by law.

Manufactured in the United States of America, or in the United Kingdom when distributed elsewhere.

Burnett, Dannella.
Visibility 4
    ISBN: 978-1-961757-79-0
    eBook: 978-1-961757-80-6

Cover design by: Jonathan Pleska
Copyediting by: Claudia Volkman
Proofreading: Sue Toth
Interior design by: Suba Murugan

speakergigs.com

CONTENTS

Foreword | Justin Guarini and Kim Walsh Phillips v

Maximizing Visibility for Impact and Income | Dannella Burnett 1

Three Fear-Busting Confidence Skills for Onstage Visibility | Diann Alexander 7

From Drifting Apart to Growing Together: Embracing Non-Traditional Love | Mark Allen 13

Breaking the Rules and Building a Business You Love | Ann Bennett 19

Unveiled Faith: The Hidden Power of Visibility | Earlene Coats 25

Breaking Free: Shaking Off the Life Others Have Envisioned for You and Finding Your Authentic Self | Mona Das 31

Relationships Are All We Got | Tim Faris 37

Seeing Your Audience from a Visionary Mindset and Perspective | Katie L. Friedman, LDO 45

Visible and Valued: What Your Employees Really Want from You | Dr. Nicholas Harvey 51

Love Among the Ruins—Peace of Mind and Happiness Are Our Birthright | Caroline Kohn, LL.B., RPC, MPCP 57

Success Leaves Clues | Jeff Marr 63

From Dimmed to Dazzling: Embracing the Power of Your Authentic Self | Lori McDowell, PhD 69

Five Steps to Relief from Overwhelm | Cecil Mcintosh 75

Integrity, Honesty, Visibility | Dr. Sree Meleth 81

Are You Too Smart for Your Own Success? | Nancy Michieli 87

Visibility IN Action: Be Seen, Be Heard, Be the Change, Lead the Change | Drocella Mugorewera 93

Take Charge of Your Healthcare: Three Roadblocks to Overcome for Safer Care! | Cathy Otten, RN, BSN 99

Is Your Weight Keeping You Invisible? | Ann Rolle 105

The Secret Sauce for Modern CEOs: Combining Post-Soviet Grit with Michelin-Star Precision for Business Excellence | Natalie Runoff 113

$avvy Style: Your Shortcut to Success | Arlene Stearns 121

Messaging Is Your Marketing—Claim Your Authentic Self for Better Clients | Kimberly Weitkamp 127

The Comeback—Reclaiming Your Sassy Spirit | Shaye Woodward 133

FOREWORD

One speech can change everything.

That simple truth is at the heart of *Visibility*, a book masterfully brought together by Dannella Burnett. In these pages, you will meet extraordinary voices who have harnessed the power of public speaking to transform their lives, their businesses, and the lives of countless others. This book isn't just a collection of strategies or tips; it's a roadmap to a new way of thinking about the spoken word—a way that's deeply rooted in impact, influence, and legacy.

As we reflect on our own speaking journeys, the idea that "one speech can change everything" is a sentiment that hits close to home. We, too, began with just a dream. There were no sold-out arenas or international flights on our calendars in the early days like there are today. In fact, there were barely any calendar events at all—just small rooms, a handful of eager listeners, and a burning desire to share our messages with the world. But that's the beauty of mastering the stage: no matter where you begin, the journey has the potential to create life-altering impact.

When we first connected with Dannella, it was clear that her vision aligned with ours. She understood that speaking isn't about perfection; it's about connection. It's about using your voice, no matter how polished or raw, to inspire, educate, and move people to action. Her passion for helping others step into their power as speakers is the driving force behind this book, and it's an honor to be a part of that mission.

The speakers you'll meet in these pages—whether they started in humble settings like libraries or church basements or have already graced prestigious stages—share something crucial: They have all dared to take the leap. They've faced the fear of judgment, failure, and not knowing what might come next. And in doing so, they've reaped the rewards that only come from stepping into the spotlight with courage and conviction.

Just look at Tony Robbins, one of the most recognizable names in the speaking world today. He didn't start by addressing stadiums of fifty thousand people. No, he began with small workshops, speaking to groups of five to ten. Over time, his ability to connect, inspire, and grow in front of his audience turned him into a household name. His story, like so many others in this book, illustrates the truth that success on the stage starts with showing up, no matter where you're starting from.

Or think of Malala Yousafzai, who risked her life to speak out for equal rights in the face of danger. Her courage to tell her story didn't just change her own life; it changed the world. Through her words, she's inspired millions, won the Nobel Peace Prize, and remains a symbol of resilience and hope for girls across the globe.

The journey to becoming an in-demand speaker isn't paved with instant success. It's a process of discovery, a refining of your message, and a commitment to your craft. Like Olympians who hone their skills in the early morning hours, we as speakers have the unique privilege of honing our craft in front of an audience. With every talk, we grow, we learn, and we make an impact—no matter where we are on the path.

Voices like our own clients at the Elite Speakers Network—Ayo Haynes, who launched a successful coaching business by leveraging her personal story of motherhood through open adoption, and Howard Globus, whose speaking generated more than eighteen thousand dollars a month in recurring revenue for his cybersecurity business. These are real people who didn't start out as polished speakers, but through dedication and passion found their voice—and ultimately their success—on the stage.

Here's the exciting part: The speaking journey you're about to embark on, or perhaps the one you're already navigating, can be even more impactful than you realize. Speaking is a learnable skill. No one is born a great speaker. It's something you cultivate over time, step by step. The good news is that you don't need to be perfect to be powerful. In fact, some of the most successful speakers in the world started out feeling scared, unsure, and maybe even a little lost.

Both of us have been there. Kim remembers the sheer terror of making her first offer from the stage. Her stomach churned; her mind raced with doubts. She had seen the polished presentations of others, and the fear of failure felt almost paralyzing. Yet, by stepping through the fear, she discovered the incredible results that come from pushing forward, even when you don't feel ready.

Justin has had similar moments. While building his own speaking business, he was often terrified that no one would buy his course or that his message wouldn't land. The path wasn't easy, but it was worth it. Today, both of us are grateful for the courage we mustered in those early days, because it has led to the lives we now live—filled with impact, influence, and yes, financial success.

That's the message we want to leave you with as you dive into this book. You don't have to feel ready. You don't need to wait until everything is perfect. You just need to show up, right where you are, with the willingness to learn, grow, and push through the fear. The rest will come.

As you read through the powerful stories and lessons shared in *Visibility*, know that you are not alone on this journey. You have a community of fellow speakers, dreamers, and doers who have walked this path before you and are cheering you on every step of the way. Let this book be your guide, your inspiration, and your reminder that one speech truly can change everything.

And Dannella Burnett, thank you for being a beacon of support and encouragement for so many aspiring speakers. Your vision for this book is a gift to all of us, and we are honored to contribute to this incredible work.

Here's to stepping into the spotlight, sharing your story, and making the world a better place—one speech at a time.

With gratitude and excitement,

Justin Guarini and Kim Walsh Phillips

Kim Walsh Phillips is the founder and CEO of Powerful Professionals, a business coaching and education company. She went from 32 clients to over 11,000 in less than a year, making this one of the fastest growing companies in America and was recently named #475 in the Inc 5000.

Named "a must to read by those in business" by *Forbes* magazine, she is the bestselling author of multiple books, including *The Shift: Scale Your Business and Multiply Your Wealth without Sacrificing You*, *The Ultimate Guide to Instagram for Business*, and *The No B.S. Guide to Direct Response Social Media Marketing*, co-authored with Dan Kennedy. She co-hosts one of the top running business podcasts with *American Idol* Season One Alumni and twenty-year entertainment veteran Justin Guarini and has been featured on BRAVO's Below Deck. She's the behind-the-scenes secret weapon of some of the biggest names in business, including Kevin O'Leary from *Shark Tank*, Dan Kennedy, Profit First author Mike Michalowicz, Harley-Davidson, Hilton Hotels, and High Point University. Kim has spoken on stages around the world, including Dubai, Moscow, London, and across the US. She resides just outside of Atlanta, GA where you can find her DJ-ing her daughters' softball games and is fueled by faith, love, laughter, Titos, and a lot of Starbucks.

Justin Guarini's illustrious career spans nearly thirty years, making him a true icon in the entertainment industry. From captivating thirty million viewers each week on the groundbreaking first season of *American Idol* to starring in seven Broadway productions, as well as his beloved performance as the character "Lil' Sweet" in the award-winning Dr.

Pepper commercial campaign, Justin's talent and charisma have left an indelible mark, bringing joy to millions across America. Beyond his on-stage and on-screen success, Justin is a sought-after mentor and coach, dedicated to helping performers, entertainers, and entrepreneurs achieve their dreams through the Elite Speakers Network program (in partnership with Kim Walsh Phillips). His 1-on-1 and small group coaching sessions have helped high achievers and six- to seven-figure business owners enhance their storytelling skills, increase sales, and deliver exceptional service. As a keynote speaker, Justin inspires audiences across America, sharing the secrets of confidence, empowerment, and commanding stage presence. He has spoken for and been endorsed by some of the biggest brands in the industry like *Oprah*, *Good Morning America*, The Magnetic Marketing SuperConference, *The Today Show*, and the Kennedy Center. As a versatile emcee, Justin has hosted in-studio talk shows and live nationally broadcast red-carpet events for the Emmys, Tonys, and Grammys, showcasing his exceptional ability to connect with audiences. Justin prides himself on delivering a diverse, memorable, and outstanding entertainment experience. His unparalleled expertise and celebrity status make him a true authority in his field, dedicated to helping others achieve their highest potential.

MAXIMIZING VISIBILITY FOR IMPACT AND INCOME

Dannella Burnett

Visibility is more than just being seen. It's about being seen by the *right* people, in the *right* way, at the *right* time. In today's fast-paced, information-saturated world, getting noticed isn't the challenge; the challenge is making sure the attention you attract leads to meaningful connections, expanded opportunities, and increased income. Speakers must focus on the clarity of their message, knowing their ideal audience, and strategically leveraging visibility opportunities that amplify both their impact and income.

The Importance of a Clear Message

At the core of every successful visibility strategy is one critical factor: clarity. Clarity in your message is the foundation that supports everything else. Without it, even the best visibility strategies can fall flat.

A clear message is the concise and specific articulation of what you do, who you serve, and the value you offer. It should be easy to understand, memorable, and, most importantly, it should resonate deeply with your ideal audience. Many entrepreneurs, speakers, and business owners make the mistake of trying to speak to everyone. As a result, their message becomes diluted and ineffective. When you lack clarity in your messaging, it becomes harder for people to understand why they should care about you or your work.

A clear message positions you as an expert in your field. It allows you to stand out from the crowd, making it easier for people to understand how you can help them. It builds trust and credibility, both of which are essential for generating income and impact. When you communicate your value clearly, people are more likely to trust you, hire you, or buy from you because they feel confident that you can solve their problem.

Consider your message as a lighthouse guiding ships safely to shore. If your light is dim or constantly shifting directions, ships will pass by without noticing or may even crash. However, if your light is bright and steady, the right ships will find their way to you. That's the power of a clear message.

Knowing Your Ideal Audience

Once you have clarity in your message, the next critical step is identifying your ideal audience. Knowing who your message is for is essential to gaining visibility that matters. Visibility without purpose can be a wasted effort. Not all exposure leads to growth. You can spend hours, even days, speaking to the wrong people and see little to no return on your time and energy.

Your ideal audience is the specific group of people who are most likely to benefit from your message, products, or services. They are the people who share a need, problem, or desire that you can address. These individuals will resonate with your message because it speaks directly to their pain points, aspirations, and values.

To identify your ideal audience, ask yourself these questions:

- Who can benefit the most from what I offer?
- What specific problem am I solving for them?
- What are their biggest challenges or goals?
- Where do they spend their time (online or offline)?
- What stage of life or business are they in?

Knowing the answers to these questions helps you avoid the scattershot approach of trying to speak to everyone. It allows you to tailor your messaging and visibility efforts to reach those who are most likely to engage with you and convert into clients, customers, or partners.

When you know your audience intimately, you can craft your message in a way that speaks directly to their needs. This connection is what creates loyalty and long-term relationships. It's the difference between someone hearing your message and feeling indifferent versus hearing your message and feeling like you are speaking *directly* to them.

A well-defined audience also helps you choose the best platforms for visibility. For example, if your audience consists of corporate executives, LinkedIn may be a better platform than Instagram. On the other hand, if you're targeting young creatives, visual platforms like Instagram or TikTok might be more effective.

Visibility: Amplifying Impact and Income

Once you have a clear message and a deep understanding of your ideal audience, visibility becomes the vehicle that amplifies both your impact and income. Strategic visibility means showing up where your audience already is, delivering value, and positioning yourself as a go-to authority in your niche.

Visibility isn't just about the quantity of exposure but the *quality* of that exposure. Being visible in front of the right audience can change the trajectory of your business and personal brand. There are numerous visibility opportunities that can be leveraged to build your presence, including live and virtual stages, podcasts, summits, conferences, TV, radio, and even hosting your own events.

1. Live and Virtual Stages

Speaking on stages, whether in person or online, is one of the most powerful visibility tools. It allows you to share your expertise with an audience in real time, creating an immediate connection and authority. Live events are great for building personal rapport, but virtual stages have opened up the possibility to reach a global audience from the comfort of your own space.

When selecting live or virtual stages, consider where your ideal audience will be. Industry-specific conferences, niche workshops, or summits related to your field of expertise can be excellent places to showcase your knowledge. The key is to be selective and intentional about the stages you choose, ensuring they align with your audience and message.

2. Podcasts

Podcasts have surged in popularity as a medium for sharing information and stories. They offer a unique opportunity to reach your audience in a more personal, intimate way. By being a guest on podcasts that align with your message and audience, you can tap into existing listener bases and share your insights in a conversational format. Podcast listeners tend to be highly engaged, making them more likely to follow up on calls to action such as visiting your website, purchasing a product, or joining your mailing list.

The beauty of podcasts is that they are evergreen content. Once an episode is published, it lives online indefinitely, allowing new listeners to discover you long after the initial release.

3. Summits and Conferences

Participating in or hosting a summit or conference is another excellent way to expand your visibility. These events typically bring together thought leaders and professionals within a particular industry or niche. By positioning yourself as a speaker or panelist, you can share your expertise with a large, targeted audience and network with other influencers and potential collaborators.

Online summits, in particular, have become increasingly popular and allow for global reach without the cost or travel associated with in-person events. Hosting your own summit or event can also position you as a leader in your field, further solidifying your authority and expanding your network.

4. Television and Radio

Television and radio, though more traditional, are still powerful tools for building visibility, especially when targeting specific demographics that consume media in this way. Local news segments, talk shows, and industry-specific radio programs can offer substantial credibility and provide a platform for reaching new audiences. These media appearances can also be repurposed across your digital platforms, giving them additional longevity.

5. Hosting Your Own Events

Creating and hosting your own events, whether workshops, webinars, or retreats, offers the ultimate control over your message and the audience you attract. Hosting events allows you to curate the entire experience, from the content you deliver to the people you invite. It positions you as a leader and creates an opportunity for direct interaction with your audience, which can build deeper relationships and trust.

Hosting your own events also opens doors to monetization opportunities, from ticket sales to upselling services or products. It's a strategy that not only amplifies your impact but can also create significant income.

Maximizing Visibility to Grow Impact and Income

Visibility, when done correctly, is more than just a marketing strategy. It is a tool for growth, both personally and professionally. To maximize the impact of your visibility efforts, consistency is key. Show up regularly on the platforms that matter to your audience, engage with them authentically, and deliver value each time. The more your audience sees you providing value, the more they will trust you and the more likely they are to invest in what you have to offer.

Visibility also increases your authority in your industry. When you consistently show up in spaces where your audience already is, you begin to be seen as an expert or thought leader. This positioning leads to more opportunities—from speaking engagements to collaborations, partnerships, and increased income streams.

Visibility, when approached with a clear message and a well-defined audience, has the potential to transform your business and personal brand. It is the catalyst that takes your expertise and amplifies it in a way that reaches the people who need it most. By leveraging visibility opportunities such as live and virtual stages, podcasts, summits, TV, radio, and hosting your own events, you can position yourself for long-term success. The key is to be intentional and strategic in how you show up, ensuring that every visibility effort aligns with your message, audience, and ultimate goals. The result? Greater impact, stronger connections, and a significant boost to your income.

Dannella Burnett is the owner of Encore Elite Events and Speakers Need To Speak. As seen in *Entrepreneur.com Magazine*, *USA Today*, *LA Tribune*, and on hundreds of stages around the world, Dannella has grown her own seven-figure business through speaking, events, and publicity and helps her clients do the same. Through her connections, millions of dollars have been generated and tens of thousands of lives impacted through speaking and live events!

speakersneedtospeak.com

THREE FEAR-BUSTING CONFIDENCE SKILLS FOR ONSTAGE VISIBILITY

Diann Alexander

There are so many heart-centered entrepreneurs, speakers, and coaches who are absolutely brilliant. Their skills and talents are so needed to uplift our world, to share new ways of healing and prosperity. We truly need them to build bridges in a world that feels chaotic and polarized. Authentic communication is essential today more than ever. Yet why are we not seeing them? Instead of brightly visible, why are so many excellent speakers still the best-kept secrets?

Simply put, it doesn't matter how good the message is if the messenger can't get on the stage.

Do you know anyone who suffers with stage fright? If the number-one fear is public speaking, and 77 percent of the population suffers from it, chances are pretty good you do.

So, are we going to let a few stage nerves get in the way of our mission? Not on my watch! In this chapter, I'm going to break down the stage fright monster and give you three actionable, fear-busting confidence skills so you can join the ranks of visible change makers creating impact and income.

When practiced, these skills can move you from nervous to noteworthy in moments. These skills have been success game changers for thousands of my students, from professional tax educators to Broadway performers. These skills are also useful in interviews, in auditions, in challenging conversations, and when dealing with big emotions like anger or grief.

Back Story

Like many of us, I grew up in a fairly turbulent household, so my MO was to make myself really small. Be the perfect daughter. Never inflame the big people. That worked pretty well for me until college.

In college, the head of the music department told me I needed to take voice lessons. Yikes! I was the composer behind the scenes; I didn't do solos! But was I going to tell him no?

I thought voice lessons would be the worst thing. It wasn't. There were these horrific things at the end of the semester called *juries*. A jury is where you had to sing in front of the faculty for a grade. And for some reason, they thought I belonged in the *public* jury! All of the students, all of the faculty, and all of their friends and family.

The day for the jury came. I remember clutching my books tightly and shuffling down that *looong* center aisle to the grand piano. There were people on the left and people on the right all looking at me. My mom said she could see my knees shake from the back of the room.

All kinds of thoughts flashed through my head. *What if they find out I've never done this before? What if I forget everything I'm supposed to do? What if they criticize me, tell me I'm not good enough, kick me out of the department? What if I let everybody down? The faculty? My parents? Myself?*

I don't remember very much else about that jury. What I do remember is that I never wanted to feel that way again. Can any of you relate to this?

Astonishingly, in college, no one addressed stage confidence. The three suggestions were:

1. "Imagine them in their underwear." There are just some things you can't unsee that do not help keep your focus on your material . . .
2. "Practice until you can't get it wrong." Well, that's a great place to start *as long as you're in the practice room*. The minute you get onstage, there are lights, different acoustics, an audience, and many more unexpected distractions. It's another experience altogether.
3. "Go! Go! Go! Go!" Translation: get onstage really fast, as though pumping up the energy was going to make you forget you were nervous. As an introvert, that was like pouring gasoline on a fire.

The Nature of the Beast

None of these three suggestions worked for me. Why didn't they work? They didn't work because **you can't paint over panic**.

The missing piece is to understand the nature of the beast. The subconscious brain's job is to keep you safe. It doesn't know if there's a real bear, a not-good-enough bear, or a what-if-they-don't-buy-my-stuff bear. It just knows you're in trouble.

So it triggers the emergency alarm, overrides the conscious brain, and diverts all your energy to the body parts that are going to get you out of danger the quickest. It's a **physical survival response** to a perceived danger.

Most speakers first go to a mindset tool. However, under the duress of perceived danger, thinking is not going to be the subconscious's first line of defense. Instead, the emergency fight-flight-fawn-fear response "hijacks your brain" to get you out of perceived trouble. Did you ever try to think away an emotion? How did that work for you?

The Conundrum

I often wonder where would I be today if I'd actually learned confidence skills alongside my performance skills. What more might I have been able to do if I hadn't spent so much time in worry, procrastination, or full-on avoidance?

What would have been different if there had been a safe, supportive environment to work through and transform those fear responses? What if I had developed strong confidence habits that became second nature?

What would be easier today? Sales conversations? Follow up? Actually stepping on the stage? How many more stages might I actually have been on? How many more sales conversations might I have actually enjoyed? How many more lives might I actually have touched?

Are you ready for some good news?

Three Fear-Busting Confidence Skills

Skill #1: Bobble Neck

Since fight-and-flight is a physical response, let's start with a physical tool. The first thing that happens when the stage monster "gets us" is the top pivot joint where the top of your neck goes into your head contracts and your breath "freezes."

Try this:

Contract your neck, then try to inhale. It's really hard!

Now, bobble your neck like those little spring dolls on the dashboard of cars, and inhale. Easier, right?

Skill #2: Add the Belly Breath

Take your hands, put them on your low, low belly, where a bikini or a speedo would be. Bobble your neck, inhale down to your hands. Push your belly out against your hands. Hold for five to fifteen seconds. Relax.

Now, inhale through your nose, bobble your neck, and with hands on your low belly, hold it, let it feel good, let it stretch open, then relax and sigh.

Congratulations! You've activated your parasympathetic nervous system. That's the calm-you-down response we want.

Skill #3: Through the Eyes of Love

In church, we had a tenor soloist named Fred. When Fred had a solo, he would walk out with his robes flowing, stand in front of the congregation, and before he opened his mouth, you could hear a pin drop! Everybody loved Fred!

One day, I got my courage up and asked him: "Fred, everybody loves you! What do you do?"

I'll never forget what he said. "Oh, it's easy. As I walk onstage, I look out at each person and send them love. I send them gratitude. I thank them for being here and celebrating with me. *I send them love.* And then, I sing."

This was a revelation to me! Here I was, just out of college with the plastered-on smile, my shoulders up around my ears, thinking, *Please like me! Please like me! Don't mess up!* Yeah, it's not the same thing.

The next week was my solo. I decided to try Fred's idea. As I walked out onstage, I made eye contact with as many people in the audience as I could, mentally and energetically sending them love. The strangest things began to happen. My shoulders started to relax. My breath started to get deeper. My emotions started to calm, and I actually could see the individuals in the audience looking warmly back at me.

This was the first time I'd ever experienced an energetic connection with the audience. That was the missing piece! Extraordinary! Why did it happen? Because I wasn't all tied up in me and my fear. I was gratefully sending them love.

Final Thoughts

If I stopped right here and you never heard another word from me, you now have tools that can change your onstage life forever. They certainly did for me and have for thousands of my clients.

What would you achieve without stage fright holding you back? Imagine the visible impact on your business if nerves didn't stop you from making those calls. How would it feel to *enjoy* getting on the stage?

It's time to find out!

Your skills and talents are so needed to uplift our world, to share new ways of healing and prosperity. We truly need to build bridges in our chaotic and polarized world. Authentic communication is essential; however, it doesn't matter how well-crafted or how important the message is if the messenger can't get onstage.

Practice the experience of loose neck, deep belly breaths, and connecting to your audience through the eyes of love and gratitude. Your visibility will increase, and you will have their attention before you even say a word.

You matter. Your voice matters. Your message matters. Let's get them out there.

Diann Alexander is a confidence catalyst, public speaker, voice and performance coach, and four-time Amazon bestselling author who has been teaching on university and professional stages for more than fifty years. If ever there was a resource to help heart-centered entrepreneurs, speakers, and coaches transform stage fright into stage confidence, Diann is it.

diannalexander.com

FROM DRIFTING APART TO GROWING TOGETHER: EMBRACING NON-TRADITIONAL LOVE

MARK ALLEN

Have you ever felt like you're following an invisible script in your relationship?

You know, that unspoken rulebook that dictates what love looks like, feels like . . . how we're supposed to be in relationship?

I'll bet you have!

We all do!

It's as if society handed us a relationship manual, and we've been trying to follow it to the letter.

But here's the thing: What if that manual is outdated?

Let's face it—with divorce rates hovering around 60 percent, it seems like the traditional model doesn't work for everyone. It's almost as if we set ourselves up for heartbreak from the start.

I remember the moment this reality hit home for me. I was six years old, heading to the kitchen for breakfast, when I stumbled upon several packed suitcases by the front door. My dad was leaving, and soon after, my parents divorced. That moment planted a seed of curiosity in my young mind: Are there other ways to approach love and relationships?

Fast-forward to my awkward high school years (and trust me, they were awkward). I was the quintessential shy, nerdy kid who couldn't even muster up the courage to talk to girls, let alone ask them out. I felt like

I was missing out on so many opportunities to connect and explore, but I just couldn't take the first step.

Then came college and my first (and only) blind date. Picture me: a bundle of nerves, my knees shaking so hard I thought they might fall off. I half expected to vibrate right off my chair! But when she walked in, something magical happened. The conversation flowed effortlessly, and now, nearly forty years later, we're still together.

Our wedding in Hawaii was like a scene from a movie: palm trees, ocean breezes, feet in the sand. Perfect, right? Well, almost. I had this nagging feeling—a little voice wondering if there was something between being single and married. At the time, I'd never even heard of non-monogamy. It was like trying to imagine a color I'd never seen before.

As the years went by, Beth and I found ourselves drifting apart. We weren't fighting, but we both knew something was missing. That spark, that excitement we once had, seemed to have dimmed. We were going through the motions, like two ships passing in the night, each on our own lonely journey.

That's when curiosity led me to discover non-monogamy through a podcast about swinging. It was like stumbling upon a hidden door in a house I thought I knew every inch of. Suddenly, there was a whole new world of possibilities I'd never considered previously.

Now, I'll be honest, my first attempt at broaching the subject with Beth was . . . less than compassionate. Let's just say that suggesting your wife listen to specific podcast episodes about swinging isn't exactly the most romantic gesture. It's about as subtle as a neon sign in a library! It caught her off guard and could have easily led us down the path to divorce.

But instead of giving up, we decided to open up—*to each other*. We worked on ourselves individually; we saw counselors and coaches. I even attended a men's retreat to connect with my masculinity. Beth started exploring her own needs and desires. It was like we were both embarking on separate journeys of self-discovery only to find that these paths led back to each other.

As we grew closer again, I found the courage to bring up the topic once more. This time, it was a casual conversation on the couch, my head in her lap, when I suggested finding a group of couples to go dancing with. Beth saw right through me and asked if I still wanted to explore swinging. I looked her in the eyes and said, "Yes, I really do!"

To my surprise, this time she was open to it. We had done so much work on ourselves and our relationship that there was enough trust to consider exploring new ways of connecting. We had built a strong foundation for our relationship, and now we felt secure enough to add some exciting new rooms to our metaphorical house.

So, we booked a trip to a clothing-optional resort in Cancun.

Talk about diving in headfirst! There we were, two middle-aged suburbanites, about to bare it all—literally and figuratively. I'd be lying if I said I wasn't nervous. What if I got sunburned in places that had never seen the sun before? But beneath the nerves was an undercurrent of excitement and anticipation.

While we didn't connect intimately with anyone else on that trip, something profound happened. We opened up more to ourselves and to each other. There was a newfound freedom and expression. Standing there, physically and emotionally naked, we realized there was nothing left to hide. We had reached a place where we could truly be honest with each other.

From there, we started attending parties and gatherings, finding friends with similar desires. And you know what? The more we opened our relationship, the better our communication became. We could talk about anything and everything. Our trust deepened because we had to prioritize our relationship as we explored new connections.

This journey has brought a renewed sense of confidence to both of us. We get to feel that rush of excitement from meeting new people, and we bring that energy back to our relationship. It's like adding fuel to a fire. Suddenly, we were both glowing with a new vitality, a zest for life and love that we thought we'd lost.

Now, I help other couples navigate this journey. I guide them in opening up about their desires in a way that honors their relationship, and we work on challenging ingrained beliefs about relationships. It's crucial to start with a game plan, setting ground rules and boundaries that both partners are comfortable with. And remember, these rules can evolve as you grow and explore.

There are many types of non-monogamy, from monogamish to polyamory and everything in between. Think of it as a buffet of relationship styles—you can sample a bit of everything until you find what works best for you!

But let me be clear: This journey isn't always smooth sailing. There are challenges, moments of doubt, and yes, sometimes jealousy rears its head. It's not about eliminating these feelings but learning to navigate them together. It's about growing together, supporting each other, and continually choosing your partner even as you explore connections with others.

I remember the first time Beth went on a solo date. I was a bundle of nerves, pacing like an expectant father in an old sitcom. But when she came home, glowing with excitement and eager to share her experience with me, I felt something unexpected—joy. Joy for her happiness, and a deepening of our connection as she shared this part of herself with me.

That's the beauty of ethical non-monogamy; it's not about replacing your partner or finding someone "better." It's about expanding your capacity for love, exploring different facets of yourself, and bringing that growth back to your primary relationship.

One of the most beautiful things I've witnessed in this journey is how it can bring out hidden aspects of your partner. I've seen shy, reserved people blossom into confident, radiant beings. And I've seen couples rediscover the spark that first brought them together.

And it's not just about the excitement of new experiences. It's about deepening your connection with your primary partner. It's about fostering a level of honesty and openness that many monogamous couples never achieve. When you can talk openly about attraction to others, when you can support your partner's growth and exploration, it creates a level of trust that's truly profound.

So, if you're feeling that pull toward something different, know that you're not alone. It's okay to question the status quo and explore new ways of connecting. Who knows? You might just find a deeper, more fulfilling love than you ever thought possible.

Love is not a finite resource. The more we open our hearts, the more love we have to give. Just like a garden— the more you tend to it, the more it grows and flourishes. And just like a garden, your relationship needs constant care, attention, and sometimes, a willingness to try new things.

Non-monogamy isn't a magic fix for relationship problems. It won't solve underlying issues or miraculously improve a struggling partnership. In fact, it will shine a spotlight on the cracks of your foundation and probably widen them. But for couples who are already strong, who communicate, and who are willing to put in the work, it can open up a world of possibilities.

It's about creating a relationship that truly reflects who you are and what you want, rather than conforming to societal expectations. It's about writing your own rulebook for love, one that honors your unique desires and needs.

So, whether you're just curious about non-monogamy or you're ready to dive in, remember this: there's no one right way to love. Your journey is uniquely yours. Embrace it, learn from it, and let it transform you.

Mark Allen is a certified transformational and heart coach with more than thirty-two years of personal experience in long-term relationships. Having navigated transitioning his own marriage to ethical non-monogamy, Mark helps couples transform their partnerships into vibrant, fulfilling connections that not only survive but thrive through the profound experiences of intimacy and exploration.

openingus.com

BREAKING THE RULES AND BUILDING A BUSINESS YOU LOVE

Ann Bennett

Let's get one thing straight right off the bat: Playing by the rules is for the boring, the mediocre, and the invisible. If you're here to blend in, play nice, and hope someone notices your perfectly curated brand, let me save you some time: That strategy sucks. But if you're ready to set fire to the rulebook, liberate your rebel spirit, and watch the money roll in, then buckle up. This is where we get loud, proud, and unapologetically ourselves.

"Unleash your inner rebel and rake in the revenue" isn't just some cute phrase. It's your new mantra. You've got something powerful inside of you, but if you keep hiding behind a mask of "professionalism" or blending into the sea of sameness, you're going to be stuck hustling for scraps while others rake it in. So, if you're ready to stop playing small and start cashing in on what makes you uniquely YOU, keep reading.

In this chapter, we're diving into why authenticity, disruption, and ditching the status quo are the keys to creating a killer brand that makes emotional waves, slaps people in the face with its boldness, and, oh yeah, brings in that sweet, sweet revenue.

Step 1: Ditch the Cookie-Cutter BS and Embrace Your Weird

You know what the most tragic thing is? Watching brilliant entrepreneurs, coaches, healers, and creatives water themselves down to fit into some imaginary box of "professionalism." Like, who came up with this idea that we all have to be beige and boring to succeed? I mean, have you ever walked into a room full of cookie-cutter professionals and thought, "Wow, this is inspiring"? Nope. You probably felt like you were drowning in a sea of beige blazers and buzzwords.

Here's the deal: Your rebel spirit is your superpower. It's what makes you different, exciting, and memorable—trying to be like everyone else? That's a one-way ticket to becoming just another voice in the crowd that nobody listens to. Your weirdness, your quirks, your bold ideas—that's the stuff that people will remember.

Think about it. If you walk into a convention full of soft-spoken healers, all draped in flowy bohemian garb, but you strut in wearing a sleek black leather jacket and a confident smirk, who's going to get noticed? You are. Not because you're trying to be a jerk, but because you're showing up as YOU. And that's the point. You can't make waves by playing in the shallow end.

Embrace what makes you different. Your rebel spirit isn't something to tame or hide; it's the secret weapon that sets you apart in a crowded marketplace. When you stop trying to be "normal" (whatever that means) and start showing up as your boldest, most authentic self, you'll start attracting the kind of clients who vibe with YOU, not the watered-down version of you. And that's when the magic (and money) starts flowing.

Step 2: People Don't Buy What You Do; They Buy How You Make Them Feel

Newsflash: Nobody actually cares about what you do. Harsh? Maybe. But it's true. People don't give a damn about your services, your fancy credentials, or your shiny website. What they care about is how you make them *feel*.

Apple doesn't sell computers; they sell creativity and innovation. Tesla doesn't sell electric cars; they sell the feeling of being part of the future. And you? You're not selling coaching, real estate, or healing sessions. You're selling transformation, confidence, empowerment—whatever it is that you help people achieve on a deep emotional level.

If your brand isn't tapping into people's emotions, it's falling flat. Period. You can have all the experience in the world, but if you don't

BREAKING THE RULES AND BUILDING A BUSINESS YOU LOVE 21

make your audience *feel* something, you're just noise. Want to be more than noise? Start showing people why they should care. Connect with them on a human level. Get them to buy into the experience of working with you, not just the service you offer.

This is where your rebel spirit comes in again. When you're real, raw, and unapologetically yourself, people feel that. They trust you more. They connect with you more deeply. And guess what? When people feel connected to you, they're way more likely to open their wallets.

Step 3: Experience Is Overrated, Personality Is Everything

If you think people choose you because of your years of experience or fancy credentials, I've got some bad news. No one cares. That's not what's bringing in the business.

We live in a world where charisma, personality, and boldness trump expertise almost every single time. Have you ever seen someone with way less experience than you raking in clients and wondered how the hell they're doing it? It's because they've mastered the art of connection. They've got energy that pulls people in. They've got a brand that stands out because it's full of personality, not just bullet points on a resume.

Look, having knowledge and experience is great. But don't let that be the thing you lead with. Lead with who you are. Lead with the energy you bring. People don't want to work with a robot who has a laundry list of credentials—they want to work with someone who gets them, who makes them feel seen, heard, and understood.

When you show up with your rebel spirit, owning your personality, and letting your freak flag fly a little, people will be drawn to you. They'll want to work with you not just because you know your stuff, but because they feel like you're the person who can take them where they want to go. And that's priceless.

Step 4: Be Loud, Be Bold, and Disrupt the Hell Out of Your Industry

Let's talk about the elephant in the room: Standing out in today's market is tough. Everyone and their mother is online, and they're all shouting for attention. So how do you rise above the noise? Easy. You get louder, bolder, and more disruptive.

This doesn't mean causing chaos for the sake of it—it means being strategic with your disruption. You need to create what I like to call a "boom effect." Something that makes people stop in their tracks and say, "Whoa, what's that all about?"

Maybe it's your marketing, your visuals, your message, or your approach. Maybe it's taking a controversial stance on an issue everyone else is too scared to touch. Whatever it is, your goal is to shake things up and make people notice. And yeah, it might ruffle a few feathers along the way, but guess what? That's a good thing. Feathers need ruffling.

Brands that play it safe and toe the line never make a lasting impact. If you want to be unforgettable, you've got to be willing to stir things up a little. And the best part? When you embrace disruption, you start attracting people who are just as bold as you. These are the clients who will love you, refer you, and keep coming back because they know you're not like everyone else.

Step 5: Differentiate or Die

If you take one thing away from this chapter, let it be this: Differentiate or die. Dramatic? Sure. But true. If you're not standing out, you're blending in. And if you're blending in, you're losing money. Period.

Your rebel spirit isn't just a cute concept—it's your differentiator. It's what makes you memorable. It's what makes people choose YOU over the sea of others doing the same thing. Your job is to figure out what makes you different, amplify the hell out of it, and make sure your audience knows exactly why they should choose you over anyone else.

This means getting super clear on your brand. What do you stand for? What do you absolutely *not* stand for? What makes you uniquely qualified to help your clients? (Hint: it's probably not your credentials.) Own your difference, and don't be afraid to shout it from the rooftops.

Conclusion: Cash In on Your Rebel Spirit

So, what's the takeaway here? It's simple: If you want to stand out, succeed, and rake in the revenue, you've got to unleash your inner rebel. Stop playing it safe. Stop trying to blend in. And for the love of all things holy, stop hiding behind the idea that your credentials are the key to success. They're not.

Your rebel spirit is your golden ticket. It's what makes people stop, notice, and choose YOU. When you embrace it, amplify it, and show up authentically, you'll create a brand that not only turns heads but also drives results. So go ahead, break the rules, shake things up, and watch the cash roll in.

Ann Bennett, founder of Renegade Branding, helps entrepreneurs build bold, stand-out brands. With more than twenty-five years of experience, she's a bestselling author and speaker who has shared stages with industry icons like Les Brown and Jack Canfield. Her mission? To unleash your rebel spirit and skyrocket your profits.

annbennettmarketing.com

UNVEILED FAITH: THE HIDDEN POWER OF VISIBILITY

EARLENE COATS

The biggest shift in my business came when I stopped hiding my faith online. From that moment, anyone who knew me in person or online knew where I stood in my faith. But the real transformation occurred when I made the decision to exclusively serve Christian women business leaders. Declaring that I serve Christian women leaders changed everything.

Suddenly, I was connecting with the right people. While it's not entirely accurate to say I only serve Christian women, I do focus my marketing on them. This clarity in who I serve and how I present myself not only shifted how others perceived me but also changed my confidence in the way I show up. Although my faith had been integrated in all aspects of my life, I was hiding when it came to the way you would see me on social media. I was fully integrating it into my business, my family—my entire life. For a long time, I believed in the importance of this integration, but I had been hesitant to be open about it.

Masterminds played a significant role in helping me make this shift. It wasn't just the guidance I received from others, but also the accountability and encouragement that came with being part of a like-minded community. Let me share a story to illustrate this.

I was attending an event as part of a mastermind group, and during a hot seat session, I found myself struggling with the language I used to describe who I served. I kept saying that I helped women business leaders, and the coach I was working with kept pushing me to narrow it down—suggesting that corporate leaders might be my niche.

I was resisting narrowing my audience, which is when another attendee spoke up. We were sharing a hotel room for that event, so she had heard me on the phone with a friend the night before. She asked me a pivotal question: "Why aren't you focusing on faith-filled women?"

I immediately made the change, and everyone in the room felt the shift in my energy and confidence. I realized that by not including my faith in my business identity, I was holding something back.

When I made the shift to openly declare that I served faith-filled women—eventually narrowing it to Christian women—it aligned with who I truly am. It allowed others to know exactly what I stand for. While I continue to serve people of all backgrounds, being clear about my faith brought a new level of focus and energy to my work.

This kind of clarity doesn't just benefit you; it aligns you energetically and allows you to have a bigger impact. The power of being clear about who you serve is not about excluding others—it's about focusing your energy and words to speak directly to the right people.

In my work, I help women turn their side hustles into full-time legacy businesses. This begins with getting clear on who they serve, just as I did. But it goes deeper. I help them identify the obstacles holding them back from stepping into the fullness of who they were created to be. Whether it's external challenges or internal doubts, these roadblocks can prevent us from realizing our full potential.

Four Keys to Clarity

1. Dream big. Stephen Covey's advice to "begin with the end in mind" is crucial here. When you know where you're going, you can map out the steps to get there.
2. Identify the obstacles. What's holding you back? Sometimes it's a lie planted in your mind from childhood. For example, I once failed a scribble art project as a child, and that experience planted a lie in my mind that I wasn't creative. That lie held me back for years, especially in areas like writing or anything that required creativity. But recognizing these lies allows you to overcome them. Other obstacles might include pursuing goals that aren't

yours but someone else's expectations, or being overwhelmed by technology. As someone who's skilled in technology, I often help women simplify their tech needs, focusing on what's necessary to move forward without getting bogged down by complexity.

3. Shift your energy through gratitude. I remember a coach who, despite being homeless and living in a tin shed, was challenged to create a gratitude list. At first, he couldn't see what he had to be grateful for, but eventually, he found gratitude in the smallest things, like the pen in his hand. That simple act of gratitude opened up a world of possibilities. I also teach clients to express gratitude in advance for what they hope to achieve. This shifts the mind from doubt to possibility. For instance, instead of just hoping for financial success, you might say, "I'm grateful in advance for the $250,000 in my bank account." This approach makes it easier for your brain to accept and believe in future successes.

4. Identify your dream carriers. These are the people who support you and help you carry your dream forward, especially when you can't do it alone. They're not the naysayers but the ones who lift you up and keep you moving toward your God-given purpose.

Now that you have clarity, here are some practical steps you can take today:

Understand Your Unique Value Proposition: One of the first steps in transitioning from a side hustle to a full-time legacy business is understanding what makes you unique. It's not just about the products or services you offer; it's about the unique value you bring to the market. Take time to reflect on your skills, experiences, and the specific needs of the audience you want to serve. This clarity not only helps in branding but also in creating a strong foundation for your business growth.

Build a Strong Brand Identity: Your brand is more than just a logo or a catchy slogan. It's the story you tell and the experience you provide. A strong brand identity resonates with your audience, builds trust, and distinguishes you from your competitors. As you build your brand, think about how your faith and values are reflected in your business. This alignment will attract like-minded clients and customers who share your vision, making your business not just profitable but meaningful.

Create a Sustainable Growth Strategy: Many side hustles fail to transition into full-time businesses because they lack a sustainable growth strategy. It's essential to plan for growth in a way that doesn't overwhelm you or dilute your brand. This includes setting realistic financial goals, understanding your cash flow, and investing in the right areas, whether marketing, technology, or team building. A strategic plan allows you to scale your business methodically, ensuring that each step forward is solid.

Leverage Technology without Overwhelm: Technology can be a double-edged sword. On one hand, it offers tools that can automate tasks, streamline operations, and expand your reach. On the other hand, it can be overwhelming and confusing, especially if you're not tech-savvy. I specialize in helping women navigate this terrain, choosing the right tools that fit their business needs without causing unnecessary stress. Simplifying your tech stack can free up your time and energy to focus on what truly matters—growing your business and serving your clients.

Build a Support Network: No one succeeds alone. As you grow your business, it's crucial to build a support network that includes mentors, peers, and a team that believes in your vision. This network provides not only practical support but also emotional encouragement, helping you navigate the ups and downs of entrepreneurship. Surround yourself with people who uplift you, challenge you, and share your passion for making a difference. This community can be a game-changer in your journey from side hustle to legacy business.

Embrace Continuous Learning and Adaptation: The business world is constantly evolving, and staying ahead requires a commitment to continuous learning and adaptation. Whether it's new marketing trends, technological advancements, or shifts in consumer behavior, being open to change is key. I offer ongoing training and resources to help you stay current and innovative. By continuously sharpening your skills and adapting to new circumstances, you ensure that your business remains competitive and relevant.

Take Action and Stay Consistent: Dreams without action remain just dreams. The journey from a side hustle to a full-time legacy business requires consistent effort and a willingness to take bold steps. It's not always easy, but with the right mindset and support, it's entirely possible. Remember, consistency is the key to success. Small, daily actions build momentum and lead to big results over time.

Every one of us has a unique purpose and gifts that God wants to use to make an impact in the world. I hope this chapter inspires you to unveil your faith and become visible in a way that aligns with who you truly are. Remember, the moment I became visible in my faith, everything in my business shifted, and I believe it can do the same for you.

Earlene Coats is a tech-savvy, intuitive business coach. Fluent in both "geek" and English, Earlene simplifies and streamlines tech solutions and empowers Christian women to turn their side hustles into full-time, impactful legacy businesses, ensuring they start with the end in mind and implement the right solutions at the right time.

dreamupevents.com

BREAKING FREE: SHAKING OFF THE LIFE OTHERS HAVE ENVISIONED FOR YOU AND FINDING YOUR AUTHENTIC SELF

Mona Das

A moment of clarity: I was standing under a gushing stream of hot water, apple-scented shampoo running into my bleary eyes, when it hit me: *I'm going to be a senator.*

It was 2007, and I was visiting my brother in Cleveland. I didn't own a TV, so I binge-watched old sitcom reruns, news programs, and infomercials. All. Night. Long. The next morning, exhausted, I scrambled into the shower, closed my eyes as the hot water cascaded through my hair, and took a deep breath. That's when the thought popped into my head.

I quickly dressed and found my brother and his future wife in the kitchen. "I'm going to be a senator," I blurted out.

My brother, ten years younger and far more practical (he's an engineer), looked up from his cereal and laughed. He wasn't laughing at me exactly, but at the absurdity of the idea.

We're the children of Indian immigrants—half of my family are doctors, and the other half are engineers. For me to say that I was going to be a senator was absurd! Not only was it far outside the acceptable group of career choices, I didn't even know anyone in politics. Furthermore, I was killing it in my career in software sales.

And yet, standing there, I knew something inside had shifted. That single, unplanned moment was a glimmer of a truth I hadn't allowed myself to fully embrace: I was destined for something more.

Listening to the Inner Voice

You, too, may share that feeling—that sense of being meant for something bigger, of making a true difference. This is not just intuition; it's your authentic self calling you to step into your purpose. In the world of thought leadership and personal branding, understanding who you truly are is the cornerstone upon which everything else is built. Before you can craft a message that resonates with others or step confidently onto a stage, you must first connect deeply with yourself.

Too often, we suppress our most authentic desires because they don't fit the narrative others have painted for us. For many of us, we're given identities by our families, communities, or cultures—identities that may have nothing to do with who we truly are. We may excel at meeting others' standards, but inside, there's a persistent ache, a quiet voice that whispers of all the dreams and parts of ourselves we've sidelined. When we live out someone else's narrative, we betray our own potential and sacrifice the joy of becoming who we're meant to be.

Because I was totally out of my element, I ended up attending *five* different training sessions on how to run for office. These gave me a set of tools to run an actual campaign, as well as the confidence to believe I could try.

Then the 2016 election happened, and whatever spark had appeared inside of me was set ablaze. I set my sights on a congressional House of Representatives seat in 2018, and I learned some hard lessons about the political game. But I tried again, this time running for Washington's 8th district state senate seat. I ran against a Republican incumbent, making my election a long shot, but I connected deeply with the community and ended up raising more than $350,000 in seven months. To everyone's surprise (including mine), I won!

My spontaneous shower revelation marked a significant step toward embracing my authentic self—a version of me that wasn't dictated by societal norms, family expectations, or even my own fears. It was a small but powerful moment, and it taught me that our inner voice, often drowned out by the noise of external pressures, carries profound wisdom if only we dare to listen.

Discovering Your Authentic Self

Authenticity isn't just a buzzword—it's a magnetic force that draws people to you and keeps them engaged. When you know who you truly are, your personal brand becomes a genuine extension of that self-awareness. It's not about creating a persona; it's about amplifying your truth.

Imagine the most impactful speakers you've seen—they resonate not just because of their eloquence but because they speak from lived experience. This genuine expression builds trust, inspires others, and creates deeper connections that go beyond surface interactions. Only by embracing your authentic self can you make the meaningful impact you're destined to make.

The Weight of Expectations

Like many immigrant families, mine had a clear vision of a successful impact: doctors, engineers, professionals with steady, respectable careers. So when I failed to qualify for the gifted program in elementary school, my parents were mortified. From that moment on, they wrote me off as average and focused on my younger brother, who excelled in math and science. I felt overshadowed, and their judgments shaped my self-image for years.

Still hoping to please them, I initially studied chemical engineering—it was what my father told me I could be. I didn't know what *I* wanted; lacking diverse role models, I couldn't imagine anything outside the stereotypical choices. My first year of college was a disaster, with a GPA of 1.999. I had to personally beg the dean for a second chance.

My father's rating system for grades was ruthless: "A" meant alive, "B" was burial, "C" was cremation, and "D" was death. I was terrified to face his disappointment, but I finally told him that engineering wasn't for me. Surprisingly, he didn't argue; my struggles had made it clear that I needed a different path. I switched to psychology, and my academic experience improved.

Breaking Free from Others' Dreams and Reclaiming Your Narrative

Failing those early tests and struggling in a field that wasn't mine taught me a vital lesson: Living someone else's dream can derail your own. Breaking away from ingrained expectations is hard, especially when they come from loved ones. We often feel pressured to conform and believe we're only valuable if we fit certain roles. But sometimes, the greatest act of love for yourself and others is to follow your own path, even when it defies tradition.

For years, I carried the burden of feeling "not enough," allowing negative voices to shape my choices. I believed I wasn't smart, capable, or worthy because I didn't fit others' expectations. Reclaiming my narrative meant unlearning these beliefs and rewriting my story. I wasn't a failed engineer; I was someone with unique strengths that didn't fit traditional boxes! It was a slow but empowering process to recognize that I am enough as I am.

By my thirties, I was ready to live on my own terms. I sought mentors, built a supportive network, and aligned my life with my true self. Embracing my authenticity meant seeing my once-perceived weaknesses—being outspoken, empathetic, driven—as my greatest strengths. These traits weren't flaws; they were the foundation of a deeply fulfilling life that allowed me to make the impact I always dreamed of.

Now I embrace being described as "loud, brown, and proud" and "tenacious." I'm known as someone who makes it happen and gets it done. Having found my own inner genius, my life's work is to empower and guide others—particularly BIPOC women—in claiming their authentic paths and taking steps to cause the greater impact only *they* can make.

Reclaiming your narrative isn't about one dramatic leap; it's trusting your inner voice, saying no to paths that don't serve you, and stepping into your authentic self, one brave decision at a time.

Doing the Work

You don't have to wait for a profound moment in the shower to begin this journey. Identifying what stands between who you've been and your authentic self begins with asking the right questions—questions that cut through the noise of external expectations and get to the heart of your true identity.

Start by asking yourself:

- Whose expectations am I still trying to meet, and why do they hold so much power over me?
- Am I pursuing goals that genuinely excite me, or am I chasing achievements that will please others?
- In what areas of my life am I saying yes when my heart is screaming no?
- What values truly resonate with me, and are they guiding my decisions, or am I living by someone else's definition of success?
- What am I afraid might happen if I start living more authentically?

These questions are the keys to unlocking your true self, helping you strip away the layers of expectation and step into a life that feels deeply and uniquely yours.

Embracing Your Path

Finding your authentic self means shaking off the life others have envisioned for you and embracing a future of your own choosing. It's the bedrock of your visibility and influence, and it's something that you create, step by step.

As I've discovered on my own journey, it's never too late to rewrite your story. And remember: the most important approval you'll ever need is your own. So go ahead—dust off those dreams you've tucked away and take that first step toward being known as the badass you are!

Dream big!

Believe in yourself.

And keep going.

Mona Das, former Washington State senator and creator of the award-winning film *Bad Ass Women Doing Kick Ass Shit*, equips ambitious women to break through barriers and bring bold ideas to life. She empowers others to confront limiting beliefs, amplify their influence, and drive meaningful impact toward an equitable world.

canaryrevolution.org

RELATIONSHIPS ARE ALL WE GOT

TIM FARIS

Who am I to equip entrepreneurs with business and personal relational skills? My relationships are falling apart! Thinking these thoughts, I look down the mountain at my fifty-two-year journey of success and failure.

As a child, I avoid Mom's deep powerful emotions and am drawn to Dad's rational mind. This sets me up for surface relationships. It also leads to teachable, life-changing lessons.

Want to remain visible in people's memory so they don't forget you? Learn from my relationship challenges at ages thirteen, twenty-six, and fifty-two.

Living Safe

At thirteen, my passion to figure out relationships begins when I don't say goodbye to Mike and James.

Not long before moving, I practice the piano, then join my best friends at the theater. The screen takes us to "a long time ago in a galaxy far, far away . . ." My mind is blown as asteroids whiz past. My mouth is open, but no words come out, and no popcorn goes in.

My heart electrifies my skinny five-foot body with emotion. This is AWEsome! In 1977, nobody's experienced anything like *Star Wars*.

Then I move far away and never see Mike and James again. I feel nothing.

"Hey, there's grief in here," warns my soul. "And anger at Dad for moving us."

But my mind keeps me safe. "No, that's for movies. I built a bridge above that stuff."

"We need to deal with this."

"No, we're running toward new adventures . . . with a positive attitude!"

"Ok, I'll store it to deal with later."

I don't anticipate the result of avoiding grief and goodbyes. In my new school, I'm friendly but don't say hello to new best friends.

The next thirteen years propel me toward success. I work multiple jobs and fly over hurdles. Meanwhile, the piano grounds me. My mind thrusts me toward college success in business, computers, and accounting.

Then three camp counseling summers awaken my love for helping people make relationships. For some reason, I always ensure they say goodbye. Eventually, I tell my girlfriend, "I love working with people and may go to seminary."

"Tim, last year I told my mom you'll be a minister." How did she know my soul's purpose before me?

We marry, move far away to attend graduate school, and plan for kids someday. I often say, "I'll be the best minister I can be." In a hospital chaplain internship, I wonder why I don't connect with patients deeply like my colleagues seem to. Am I failing?

My mind's solution: "Think more. Work harder."

Losing My Mind, Finding My Heart

At twenty-six, I'm unstoppable! Until I walk in the door from a South Africa mission trip and my wife of three years walks out.

I share my story with fellow student ministers, hoping for validation and friends in the darkness. None are helpful. "At least you don't have children," one assures, fixing his emotions. This begins my quest to learn how to be with people in struggles.

Searching for answers in a winter fog, I fall into questions. While my mind makes me look successful, my heart gasps in oceans of grief and failure.

To save me, my soul orders, "Grab the hammer. Hit it."

My mind argues. "No. Successful people don't let stuff bother them."

"Grab! The! Hammer!" whispers the loudest force I ever encounter.

My body moves irrationally toward the picture, weapon in hand.

My life shatters.

Sitting in glass shards, our smiling faces crumpled before me, I sob. For hours.

Stuff stored deep for a quarter-century washes out in waves. For days.

The bridge built to keep me safe lies in jagged rubble. I wander in the wilderness. For weeks.

While my mind loses control, my soul begins to breathe. I become depressed so I can't fly above reality anymore. I feel everything. For months.

The piano invites me to lose my mind in the moment, repeatedly singing "The Rose." My heart cries pain about dead winter love and faith seeds blooming through snow. Someday.

One dark spring night, my voice shakes. "What was that?"

I sing out pain and hope again. "Where'd that come from? I've never had a vibrato!"

My soul whispers, "We've always had a vibrato—it was buried under twenty-six years of stuff. Finally, the path is clear to feel it."

Memories flash back to making up my ten-year-old mind. "Dad, I'm gonna quit piano."

"So you want to quit, Tim. Mom and I hear you improve every week. What if you play a little longer? You'll get better and may really like it."

Funny how quickly I change my young, determined mind. Is this my soul keeping me deeply connected?

Struggling for Balance

Summer arrives. Instead of resume-boosting jobs, my soul pulls me to the Appalachian Trail. My mind hurls me up mountains: six hundred miles in five weeks. With a broken arm!

After stopping at a pay phone to hear that the divorce is final, I run through a thunderstorm.

"Stop!" my soul implores. "We're missing sunsets, people, and ourself." The next five weeks, I slow to 370 miles, feel everything, and make friends.

The deeper I feel uncomfortable emotions, the higher I experience joy. Feeling lows and highs is an awesome contrast to my early flatline life.

Over the next twenty-six years, my mind rockets me through successes and failures. My soul tirelessly pulls me back to my heart, the source of creativity and relationship.

I lead people in churches; I direct camp and retreat centers. Helping organizations and people grow is my passion. When I connect with emotion, my speaking moves groups to action, and my listening helps struggling people. Yet, some work relationships are draining.

At home, I marry again and adopt two children. Family life is fulfilling and challenging. Years later, when family dynamics change, I work hard to fix it.

By midlife, I'm burned out at work and home.

Once, I arrive late to meet my district supervisor. He's angry, and talks for an hour. I take notes.

I'm proud of my listening skills. Last month, a therapist on my board says, "You listen well, especially with challenging people."

Suddenly, my boss says, "You're a terrible listener!" The meeting ends.

My identity story is that I am a successful leader, speaker, husband, and father. Yet these relationships are strained. My mind makes me live up to my story. But my soul knows reality.

Soon, the job ends and the marriage dissolves.

Discovering Wisdom and Relationship Frameworks

At fifty-two, I sit bewildered on this pivotal life mountain.

Who am I to help people improve relationships when mine fell apart?

My body depresses me again—a natural response to living incongruently. This "dark night of the soul" is deeper and longer than twenty-six years ago. The only way out is through.

I buy a travel piano and drive up Colorado's Rocky Mountains to ski, heal, and question. Why am I good—and bad—at relationships? What's the key? How can I help others avoid relationship pitfalls?

Voyaging deep, I heal and gain wisdom from hard lessons. I research relationship skills, brain science, and emotional connection. This quest results in three frameworks, plus practices, for transforming business and personal relationships.

RELATIONSHIPS ARE ALL WE GOT

The primary framework is SETS:

- Sensations
- Emotions
- Thoughts
- Stories

Picture these as:

1. Body sensations
2. Heart emotions
3. Head thoughts
4. Story bubbles above

The goal of a relationship is helping another feel understood. Two problems hinder this:

1. We interpret others' experiences by projecting our SETS onto them.
2. We focus on surface words/stories.

Instead:

1. Become self-aware, separating our SETS from theirs.
2. Respond to their emotions and thoughts (perspectives) so they feel understood.

Imagine a client saying, "You're not delivering on your promises. My business isn't growing." You quickly have body sensations, emotions, thoughts, and develop a story interpretation.

Usually, you respond to their story. "I've done what I promised" or "What am I not delivering?"

Instead, respond to their emotions and thoughts: "It seems you're frustrated with lower business growth than you want."

If you guess their emotions and thoughts wrong, no problem. They'll correct you. Then when they feel understood, they're ready to problem solve.

Remember the supervisor meeting? My unconscious often brings up this memory, but each time I justify my listening.

Finally, I use the SETS framework to understand. Stressed, I defaulted to childhood coping: living in my head. What if I had responded to his emotions and thoughts? "It seems you may feel disrespected by my late arrival" or "It seems this is upsetting."

He'd either agree or correct me. Since I'm trying to understand him, we may connect.

Maybe his "You don't listen" really means "I don't feel understood." After reframing this memory, it rarely returns.

Today, I'm grateful I lost my mind, found my heart, and discovered wisdom.

Want to remain visible in people's memory? Help them feel understood by responding to their emotions and thoughts. They won't forget you.

Let's improve our relationship skills.

Because . . . relationships are all we got.

Tim Faris helps entrepreneurs and leaders improve their relationship skills so business profits and impact increase, and their families light up when they get home. The founder of Relationships Are All We Got, he is a transformational speaker and coach.

relationshipsareallwegot.com

SEEING YOUR AUDIENCE FROM A VISIONARY MINDSET AND PERSPECTIVE

KATIE L. FRIEDMAN, LDO

The only thing worse than being blind is having sight but no vision.
— *Helen Keller*

Standing alongside an overhead projector, speaking about "Optics for the Mathaphobic" (fear of math) to about fifty opticians and medical assistants at the Javits Center Vision Expo in New York City, my body tingled as I acknowledged to myself that I'd made it as a speaker!

Dressed in a previously owned St. John Knit outfit, it was just the beginning of my journey as a speaker. As I replaced each transparency slide with a friendly technical, nontechnical explanation, I had a feeling of detachment, almost as if I were blind to the participants in the room. I hoped that presenting the material from a computer would allow me to be in a fully lit room and face the audience.

At that time, I knew where I wanted to go in my career. As a skilled optician, I wanted to educate others in the eyecare industry, but I wasn't yet connected to the people who could help me get there. I wanted to be known for my technical expertise rather than as a glasses fashion consultant or an assistant, like many of the women in the industry at the time. This was back in the 1980s and 1990s when I was climbing up the one-person corporate ladder.

I had picked this career because this career picked me. During a meditation session, recalling my childhood, I remembered guiding my older sister around the front yard because her eyes were patched. As an adult, I learned that she had ulcers on her corneas because she was allergic to grass.

That was not my inspiration, though. Neither was the time when I almost flunked third grade because I couldn't see the chalkboard from the back of the classroom. That back corner seat was preselected because of my last name. Apparently, I was a bit disruptive. I definitely wasn't interested in learning. I preferred playing during recess and lunchtime. Maybe it was because I couldn't see well at a distance (and didn't realize that others could see what I couldn't) and I couldn't understand what I was reading. Fortunately, my teacher advocated for me, suggesting that I get an eye exam because perhaps I needed glasses.

Two things happened: my seat was moved to the front of the classroom, and I wore pink cat-eye-shaped glasses. Not only could I see the leaves on trees at a distance, but I could also see the words on the chalkboard. And I passed the third grade!

The little voice in my head has been pretty loud sometimes: "You are such a loser," or "You're stupid." On top of it all, I had more energy than anyone in my family, and I was always getting into trouble. My mom refused to help me with homework, Dad and I had yelling duels regarding math, and my sister corrected my English homework so much so that it sounded more like her voice than mine. Still, I finally graduated high school.

In the first year of college, I went into the English instructor's office for help, and he asked how I'd come this far because I was unteachable. Continuing, he said, "Do us both a favor. Take this class credit/no-credit and never show up again." I was a good girl. I complied.

Fast-forward to the third year of college—I'm taking a physics class. To my amazement, I got an A on my optics exam and labs. My first academic A!

That night, as my dad was standing over the stove cooking something yummy, I stood in the doorway to share the good news. He said something along the lines of, "Check it out and see if you like it. The key to life is finding a career that feels like you're not working." So I did just that! I complied.

I got a job as a receptionist for a local optometrist. I read his optical books. Mind you, I still wasn't a reader, yet I was fascinated with the concept of light bending through different mediums. I also liked helping people.

That experience inspired a journey to an optical vocational college and a year of apprenticeship in different environments while taking one class in the morning and one at night.

After graduating from optical school, I got a job working for a hard contact lens manufacturing office that specialized in fitting orthokeratology and diseased eyes with contact lenses. I opened a mini-optical department, selling sunwear and filling vision prescriptions.

The next year, my career ventured to San Diego, California, where I opened and managed an optical shop for the ophthalmology department in a medical clinic. That's when I started taking more certification exams and collecting initials after my name. I felt smart for the first time in my life.

The little voice inside my head was so proud of me. I became known in the Opticians Society and in the eyecare community. Yet there was still that voice of regret that I wasn't smart enough to graduate college, since I had given up on getting a degree in environmental health and dropped out as a senior. That's why I think the eyecare industry picked me as much as I pursued it.

My career path continued to make twists and turns. As managed care changed the nature of the ophthalmology department, I shifted to being an office manager in optometry offices and a part-time contact lens specialist for ophthalmology practices.

On one vacation, I joined an international bus trip with a group of opticians in Australia. It was an excuse to travel for business. I applied to take an advanced-level exam that most people flunked the first or second time before receiving their fellowship in contact lenses. I went for the adventure and passed the written exam without any problem. At this stage, I was experienced academically and experientially.

Next, the orals. There were six or eight stations. The first examiner was very tall and very intimidating. He showed me several slides, and I couldn't identify the diagnosis for one of them. That little voice said,

"Well, you tried, and at least you got a trip out of this." I continued to the next stations stress-free, as I had already given up on myself. At that point, the oral exam was fun, and I breezed through the rest of the interview stations.

Out of the thirty or forty people sitting for the exam, I was one of six who passed. I earned Fellow status in the Contact Lens Society of America on the first sitting!

Throughout my career, I often got into trouble because I talked too much to the patients. They asked me questions about their prescriptions, so I provided answers. I felt I was doing a service for the doctor, only my superiors didn't see it that way.

Then a door opened for me to teach optical technology at Palomar Community College as part of the Regional Occupational Programs series. I taught evening classes part-time after working full-time managing an optical department for an ophthalmology group.

What a turn of events! Now I was a teacher inspiring future opticians. Through this position, I had the opportunity to continue speaking, this time paid for by the Vision Council of America. Being able to speak to both small and large groups inspired me to branch out as an optician, yet something inside was still missing.

Fast-forward again—now I was living in Honolulu, Hawaii. I built another optical department from scratch for an ophthalmology practice and managed it for about six years. I still answered patients' questions and got into trouble for spending too much time per patient. Because of my age, the doctor put me on notice, and I complied.

Next I sold high-end eyewear in an optical boutique in Waikiki before getting a job working for the state nonprofit on assistive technology for the disabled.

That job was a game changer. First, because I learned a missing piece in my portfolio: tools and resources for the visually impaired. Even more importantly, I learned about the "stupid gene" I'd lived with my whole life. There it was in black and white when a woman was talking about dyslexia and ADHD. I was sitting in the Assistive Technology booth crying and thinking, *That's me! Someone else understands the difficulty I have processing information.*

I finally understood why I see differently.

And now I see why I'm a good teacher. It's because I break down concepts to the smallest element, then build them up from there. Some students don't like my style, and now I understand why. I'm okay with that.

You see, my new vision and passion is to help one hundred thousand people see beyond their visual limitations, whether they're sighted or visually impaired. This includes speaking to entrepreneurs and businesses owners with a vision for alternative modalities for reducing stress in the workplace, increasing productivity, and tapping into hidden profitable opportunities.

One more thing: I received a bachelor of arts and sciences in vocational education from San Diego State University when I was forty-five years old!

Katie L. Friedman, LDO, is a licensed dispensing optician, contact lens expert, and low vision specialist. As an educator, speaker, and author, she is currently focusing on proactive applications for entrepreneurs and corporate leaders in increasing productivity and profits. Katie is also the author a number-one bestselling book on vision and visionary insights.

5stareyecare.com

VISIBLE AND VALUED: WHAT YOUR EMPLOYEES REALLY WANT FROM YOU

Dr. Nicholas Harvey

I am a man of substance, of flesh and bone, fiber and liquids—and I might even be said to possess a mind. I am invisible, understand, simply because people refuse to see me. Like the bodiless heads you see sometimes in circus sideshows, it is as though I have been surrounded by mirrors of hard, distorting glass.
—*Ralph Ellison,* The Invisible Man

Amahle (not her real name) is an executive coach from South Africa. I met her on the last day of an international gathering of the International Coaching Federation several years ago. As we were introduced, I made sure to pronounce her name correctly: "Pleased to meet you, Amahle." To my surprise, she became visibly emotional and began to cry. Concerned, I asked if she was all right. She dried her eyes and said, "You are the first person here to say my name correctly. I will never forget you."

What had I done? In my mind, I hadn't done anything significant. But to her, it was a precious gift. I saw her. She wasn't invisible to me, as she had been to many of our other coaching colleagues who hadn't taken the time to learn how to say her name properly. It's often said that one of the most beautiful sounds a person hears is their name pronounced correctly. In that moment, Amahle felt seen, heard, and valued.

I understand how important that is. For many years, I hid parts of myself out of fear of judgment, criticism, or envy. I've been hated simply because of who I am and because I was present. Visibility, in its truest sense, means being able to show up as your authentic self without fear of backlash and being appreciated for who you truly are.

My experience of integrating white environments began at the age of four in the American South. My history is filled with being the "first Black" in many settings. Being the *first* often meant being the *only*, and my uniqueness was rarely celebrated. In those predominantly white spaces, I learned that hospitality was not a gift freely given to all but rather extended to a select few. Not everyone was welcome.

To survive, I hid by staying off the radar and downplaying any of my abilities that might be seen as threatening or label me as an "uppity negro." I put on what Paul Laurence Dunbar refers to as "the mask that grins and lies." I was smart, but I made sure I was never the smartest. I ignored the daily insults, ignorance, and indignities directed my way. I went along to get along, feeling that this was the only choice I had to survive. Why endure such treatment? As an African American, I knew all too well the tragic history of what happened to Black people who didn't "stay in their place." Southern trees bore strange fruit.

Recently, there's been a lot of talk about authenticity in the workplace. The idea is that workers will perform better, stay longer, and be healthier if they can show up as themselves at work. Unfortunately, research shows that members of underrepresented minorities often don't feel they can. Why not? Fear.

In a survey conducted by Job Sage, more than three out of five people said they're currently hiding at least one aspect of their identity from their employer. Additionally, 64 percent said they've experienced backlash after revealing something about themselves, often being treated unkindly or ignored completely. Civility in the workplace is the new buzzword, but being merely polite isn't enough. Employees can't and won't become truly visible until they are valued—not just for their contributions to the work but for who they are as human beings.

What do you see when you look at an employee? Do you see an interchangeable part in the corporate machine, someone who can be easily replaced? Or do you see a person—a fellow traveler on this journey of life with an identity, a story, hopes, dreams, fears, and challenges just like you? Some people claim to be color-blind, saying they don't see color. But do you know what that statement communicates to marginalized individuals? It tells them you don't see them; you don't appreciate their uniqueness.

Someone once asked me, "What can leaders do to make their employees feel more included in the workplace?"

I replied, "Find ten employees you don't know well and ask them what it costs them to show up at work every day."

By doing so, leaders will discover that many of their employees from underrepresented communities pay an emotional and psychological price just to be part of the workforce. Then leaders can take action to create a more welcoming workplace where workers can be visible and valued.

What would such a workplace look like? I was traveling in the northwestern United States, conducting trainings for several municipalities on belonging. I noticed how one city's training facility had handicap-accessible ramps and automatic door openers. The restrooms were gender-neutral and also accessible.

At another city hall, I observed images that represented the full spectrum of humanity. All types of people were displayed, including indigenous peoples on whose land the city hall stood. Signs and materials were provided in multiple languages.

On another occasion, I saw a calendar that positively affirmed celebrations like Juneteenth and PRIDE Month. I recently worked on reviewing a Human Resources Workforce Policy and appreciated how the organization wanted policies that didn't discriminate against any employees in any way and instead affirmed their unique identities.

At another site, I spoke to employees about how we communicate across cultures to foster better human connections. Did you know that when we meet another human being, we're engaging with another culture? Often, our conflicts arise from our failure to communicate properly and the misunderstandings that follow.

When we are visible and valued, our communication styles are not judged inappropriately. Colleagues develop a heightened awareness of human differences, cultures, and perspectives and can appreciate these qualities without dismissing, diminishing, or disregarding them. These are several examples of elements that signal to employees that they can be visible and are valued.

I mentioned earlier a leadership approach where leaders reach out to employees they may not regularly engage with. What does this accomplish? In environments where employees feel invisible and undervalued, they also do not feel safe. Trust is the currency of leadership and is cultivated in an environment of psychological safety. By speaking to your employees and truly listening to them, they develop a sense of contributor safety and can share openly without fear of negative consequences. Visible and valued employees trust their leadership to create a safe environment where workers can be themselves.

Contrary to popular belief, the wave of voluntary resignations seen during and after the pandemic, known as the Great Resignation, has not ended. According to the Bureau of Labor Statistics, in July 2024 alone, 3.3 million workers quit their jobs. Leaders continue to struggle with recruitment, retention, and relationships—challenges that ultimately impact their revenues. Once again, what can leaders do?

Leaders are the bearers of culture in any organization. They define, shape, and sustain the culture. It's their job to create and promote safe spaces within the workplace where visibility and value are the norm. How does your organization measure up? Ask your employees—personally. Workers have been surveyed to death and no longer trust that senior leadership will act on the findings.

The personal touch, human to human, when we not only hear the responses to our questions but also listen to the stories behind the answers, creates a powerful dynamic. What do your employees really want? They want to be visible, where they can show up as their best authentic selves. And they want to be valued as human beings.

Atlanta native **Dr. Nicholas Harvey** uses his experience as a pastor, professor, and military officer to support leaders in creating welcoming workplaces where all can thrive. A leadership and organizational development consultant, strategic advisor, executive coach, and bestselling author, his work has been recognized by the *Los Angeles Tribune* and Georgia State University.

nicholasharveyconsulting.com

LOVE AMONG THE RUINS—PEACE OF MIND AND HAPPINESS ARE OUR BIRTHRIGHT

Caroline Kohn, LL.B., RPC, MPCP

A psychologist colleague of mine once said that if we've experienced a terrible event in our lives—an accident, crime, natural disaster, physical or emotional abuse, violence, war—there is something definitive we can point to as the cause of our difficulties in life. The fact that we have trouble managing our emotions, or that our relationships are strained, or that it's hard for us to feel love and joy is completely understandable.

But the vast majority of us who seek transformational change have not experienced this sort of traumatic event. The root causes of our struggles are more of a mystery; our suffering may be more hidden, though just as intense. And it may be harder to ask for help.

Maybe our marriage has gone off the rails. Perhaps we're experiencing conflict with our parents or children, our boss or coworkers that we don't know how to resolve and avoid like the plague. Maybe we feel depressed. Perhaps anxiety and worry lurk constantly in the back of our minds. Maybe we're overwhelmed and overloaded by endless to-do lists. Perhaps we've suffered losses we haven't adequately grieved. Or maybe we've endured criticism, failure, or disappointment that have eroded our confidence and self-esteem. Maybe we just feel angry or sad or scared for no apparent reason.

To anyone looking at us and our lives, *and even in our own minds,* we have all the metrics of success. We *should* be happy, but we're not. We tell no one, put on a smiley face, do our best to hide our pain, and soldier on. After all, look at what other people are going through. *What right do we have to complain?*

Complaining, blaming, and guilting ourselves are happiness thieves for sure. But whatever our life circumstances and history, we have every right to address our unhappiness in constructive ways. Indeed, we owe it to ourselves and the people we love and who love us to do what's necessary to reclaim the happiness and peace of mind that are our birthright. There is no inherent value in a life of silent suffering and quiet desperation.

> *It's not so much that we're afraid of change, or so in love*
> *with the old ways. But it's that place in between that we fear.*
> *It's like being in between trapezes. It's Linus when his blanket is*
> *in the dryer. There's nothing to hold on to.*
>
> —M. Ferguson

After thirty-plus years of providing psychological counseling and coaching services, I'm convinced that the roadmap to transformational change—reclaiming our peace of mind and happiness as our birthright—involves looking carefully at three things: what we think, what we feel, and what we do.

1. What We Think: What we think about, our mindset, beliefs, and the very subjective interpretations we give to the events in our lives and the behavior of others shape our feelings and determine our responses. We need to learn how to step back and observe our thoughts. We need to stop believing everything we think. We can then evaluate the impact of what we think on how we feel and what we do, and only then can we make good choices that take us where we want to go.

2. What We Feel: Feelings are the **heart** of change. We can't create the transformational change we want without attending to the emotional pieces. It just won't happen. We can only strive, push through, rise above, and positively affirm for so long. The lasting change we seek lies in our ability to accept the natural and normal

feelings that accompany every aspect of our lives and will certainly accompany change. We need to stretch our emotional capacity, feel whatever there is to feel, move through it, and let go. There are no shortcuts.

3. What We Do: Our thoughts determine our feelings, not the other way around. And our thoughts and feelings combine to drive our behavior. We must be willing to face up to and take responsibility for what we are ***doing*** that is not working. The good news is that right action often becomes obvious and flows naturally from right thinking and the ability to feel and release our emotions.

As smart, savvy, successful professionals, executives, and entrepreneurs, we recognize our patterns and even have a pretty good grasp of where they come from. Yet we still feel jammed up. Why? Because an intellectual understanding is a great beginning, but it isn't enough for the transformational change we seek.

If we could have figured everything out or fixed things on our own, we would have done it by now. We haven't because there is often a deep disconnect between what we know and understand in our heads, what we feel, and what we say and do.

This is why a coach or a guide can be so helpful—someone who sees the light at the end of our tunnel when we don't. Someone who can help us navigate the potholes and avoid the dead ends.

I know this journey.

I know what it's like to have things look pretty perfect on the outside and yet feel pretty wretched on the inside. I've had to walk the walk.

I had a privileged childhood in a peaceful Canadian city. But my family history is steeped in tragedy, loss, and violence. I'm quite convinced that I chose my counseling and coaching career in large part to heal myself and to save myself from the ghosts of my family's experiences.

My parents were Holocaust survivors, and frankly, I don't remember not knowing that something horrible had happened to my parents and extended family. As a young child with no context, I felt very unsafe, anxious, and insecure. My mother would occasionally speak of her experience in blurts and snippets. It was all very confusing and scary. Lurking constantly in the background was my fear of some terrible disaster striking at any moment out of nowhere. This fear haunted me well into my adulthood.

There was no one to talk to about any of it. Our family pain was shrouded in secrecy. Besides, what right did I have to complain about anything at all given what my parents had gone through?

On the outside, I was highly functional and excelled in school. I had lots of friends and was involved in many extracurricular activities. I *looked* happy. On the inside, I was an anxious wreck—insecure, afraid, lonely, and ashamed. I worried constantly. I longed for and envied what I perceived to be "normal" families.

While I was studying for the bar exam and suffering from overwhelm and lethargy, I had my first introduction to counseling and coaching. The floodgates in my heart opened wide. For the first time in my life, I talked about my fear and pain and allowed someone to bear witness to my anguish. I began to experience relief from the confusion and taste the mental freedom of clarity and peace of mind. My transformational healing began in that moment and has continued ever since in a lifetime process, as has my commitment to helping others do the same.

Maybe you've sought out lots of help that didn't really work for you in the long run, and perhaps you don't think there is anyone out there who can truly help you. Maybe you doubt there's someone knowledgeable and experienced enough, trustworthy and respectful enough, been through enough herself enough. Someone who has the right balance of compassion for your situation and the moxie to be straight and direct with you about what's involved and what it's going to take for you to make those transformational changes you so long for.

Just imagine, though, how much lighter you would feel if you were no longer plagued with overwhelm and anxiety, responsibility for everyone else's happiness, or a vague sense of guilt that no matter what you do, it's not enough.

Imagine how relieved you would feel if you could stop trying to figure everything out all by yourself. If you didn't have to worry that if you open up, your story would come back to haunt you on social media. If you could stop hiding your emotional turmoil, stop minimizing it, and start talking about it.

Imagine the confidence and faith in yourself you would have if you knew you had a toolbox full of solid and effective tools at your disposal to help you address and resolve whatever challenges life might throw your way.

I assure you that no matter what kind of mental or emotional distress you're experiencing or where it comes from, there are ways for you to address it, move through it, and get to the other side into greater happiness and peace of mind. I assure you that reclaiming your happiness and peace of mind as your birthright is indeed within your grasp.

Caroline Kohn, LL.B., RPC, MPCP, is a former family law lawyer. For the past thirty years, she has helped hundreds of women and men enjoy greater peace of mind and happiness through psychological counseling and coaching services, seminars, workshops, and public speaking engagements.

carolinekohn.ca

SUCCESS LEAVES CLUES

JEFF MARR

Starting a family at age seventeen and becoming a police officer three weeks after turning twenty-one forced me to grow up quickly. Next I hired a contractor to build a house for me on some vacant land in the mountains I had purchased. After several months of minimal production and limited communication, I decided to fire the contractor and build the house myself, so at age twenty-two, I completed a 4,800-square-foot custom home. At this time, I was a dad to two little ones with another on the way, and the house was just another feather in the cap of my adult journey. It seemed normal to me to have so much responsibility at my young age, and I had everything under control.

Or so I thought.

Witnessing death firsthand three months into being a police officer was a traumatic experience in and of itself. I crawled underneath a casino passenger bus after the driver had run over and crushed an eighty-seven-year-old woman. I held her hand as she stared into my eyes, and I watched her soul leave her body. At the time I did not realize the impact this would have on me, and I had no idea those memories would stick with me for the rest of my life.

My eight-year career as a police officer ended abruptly after some poor decisions I made while off duty, most of which were highly influenced by alcohol intoxication. As a young police officer, nobody taught me how to cope with any of the trauma I would witness. We all had an understanding that trauma was all just "part of the job," and we needed to compartmentalize things to be able to continue working. Nothing prepared me for a long career, and nothing prepared me for what life would look like as a civilian. When you spend forty-plus hours a week protecting and serving the general public, you tend to lose sight of reality.

I had six kids at the time I lost my career. I also was going through divorce, had already lost my home to foreclosure, and was in the middle of filing bankruptcy. During my tenure as a police officer, I coached sports full time and had started a business on the side. Everything seemed to take priority over being a husband and father, especially my desire to be the best police officer I could. I aimlessly walked through life feeling somewhat empty and not realizing the gifts that were right in front of me: my family.

Being forced to start life over again at age twenty-nine was a shock, to say the least. Being an alcoholic and suffering with depression, suicidal ideation, PTSD, and anxiety, I chose to bury my head in the sand, and I continued drinking heavily for years to come. All I had known as an adult was to be a police officer—to show up and help others when they couldn't help themselves—and ultimately be the calm in the storm. When I was sworn in to serve and protect, I never thought I would find myself trying to find a new path. I spent a long time grieving the loss of my career, thinking I would no longer have a positive impact on anyone else's life without the badge and uniform, and really just feeling sorry for myself. I took the unhealthy approach of drinking copious amounts of alcohol to numb the pain and drown out the noise inside my head.

I had all but given up.

I still got up, most days . . . if I wasn't drunk or nursing a hangover from the night before by drinking even more to stave off the shakes and crippling anxiety that accompanies detoxing. I also found myself many times detoxing inside of a jail cell after being arrested. Anytime I would fall, I would eventually get back up. And when I did, I always got up a little better. I always found a way to rebuild, make things successful again, and get a little bit further in life than I was prior to falling off the rails by going on a bender.

The problem that any alcoholic or addict will tell you is that until you completely put the substance down, it will creep its way back into your life. We lie to ourselves and tell ourselves we can do better this time, that we won't push it too far, that we won't go over the edge.

Over a three-year stretch, I checked myself into urgent cares or emergency rooms more than twenty-five times. Some of these instances occurred involuntarily after having seizures due to too much alcohol or detoxing. There was a handful of times that I would wake up inside an ambulance being rushed to a hospital. These were scary episodes, and I always made a promise to never go back, but when the uncomfortableness, shock, and embarrassment of whatever poor decisions I had made while drinking wore off, I would always find my way back to a bottle.

On November 28, 2023, I walked into the hospital ER and told them something was not right. I was awake the entire night prior with uncontrollable shakes and an overwhelming feeling of doom. The staff did their typical routine: they gave me some medicine, put me on an IV, and observed me for a couple of hours. Then they sent me on my way and told me I would be fine as long as I picked up the medicine that was prescribed and followed the instructions. I was used to the routine by now. I was somewhat of a pro detoxer.

I returned to my buddy's couch, where I had stayed the night before, but I couldn't stop the shakes or the overwhelming feeling of doom in my head. I knew something was terribly wrong. I made my way back to the hospital, where they somewhat reluctantly admitted me for observation.

I received visits from several of my kids and a couple close friends, all with confused and concerned looks on their faces as they watched me lying there somewhat lifelessly due to the medication designed to slow down the detoxing my body was experiencing and keep me comfortable.

On the third night in the hospital, my heart stopped.

I woke up to my charge nurse over me stating, "The patient is awake and breathing again." Moments later, my room was flooded with nurses and doctors and a crash cart. I answered the litany of questions the best I could, but I really had no idea what had just happened. I remember staring at my feet, shaking uncontrollably, and in that moment I had one overarching thought: *I was built for greatness, and I'm not gonna go out by letting a poison kill me.*

Whether you are spiritual, believe in God, or have your own faith, anyone who has been in a near-death situation has experienced something similar. God was in the room with me that night, amid the chaotic atmosphere of hospital staff trying to ensure I was all right. I felt a calming presence in the corner of the room. I knew something was there; I saw it with my spirit. The message that came to me was simple and delivered in an empathetic, pure, and understanding way: "We got this, buddy. As soon as you're ready to put it [alcohol] down, we have big things to do. I'm not gonna let you get off that easy; we have big things to do."

In that moment of clarity, I knew I would never go back to drinking alcohol and allowing that poison to take my life.

The months following this incident were nothing less than miraculous. Everything in my life changed; everything got better. I didn't touch a sip of alcohol and saw my life flourish around me. I was able to get into a house, which was a huge upgrade from merely renting a bedroom from a friend. I joined forces with a friend in his business, working for his company for several months and getting established again. I restarted my own company, along with several others, and saw blessings after blessings take place. It was an overwhelming sign that I am, in fact, built for greatness, built to help, and built to thrive.

Getting up every day and showing up has been the greatest blessing of my life. I have been able to impact numerous people through my speaking and coaching and have been able to find a new passion for life and helping others again. I have found a new identity outside of police work and reaped rewards I had previously only imagined.

At the end of the day, I rest easy knowing these things: We all go through struggles—we all have bumps in our journeys—but we all have the opportunity to get up and make a better life. The true sign of someone's impact in this world is not how we start our journey but how we finish it.

I'm living proof that we can all finish strong. If we are still alive and still breathing, we still have purpose and an opportunity to do more.

Jeff Marr is the father of seven children, a mental performance coach, inspirational speaker, author, and entrepreneur based in the Denver area. Jeff has dedicated his life to helping others realize their potential through proper mindset and breaking through limiting beliefs.

www.mevme.org

FROM DIMMED TO DAZZLING: EMBRACING THE POWER OF YOUR AUTHENTIC SELF

LORI MCDOWELL, PHD

As a very young child, visibility was my middle name. Being the first child, the first grandchild, the first niece in a very close family, my natural tendency to shine was encouraged. I would sing, dance, be the center of attention, the princess. My uncle Mikey, the amateur photographer, took hundreds of photos of me, and I was happy to pose. I would talk to anyone and always had something to say. My mom even entered me in the Little Miss America Pageant. I loved being visible, being on stage, and letting my true self shine!

Somewhere around age five, something changed. My sister was born, and we moved to the suburbs. I started kindergarten. I realized that my name rhymed—I was Lori Torry. I went from being an adorable toddler who was often compared to Shirley Temple to a smart, chubby child with a bad haircut. I still put myself out there, yet not nearly as much. At times I found myself hiding, trying to fade into the background. Teachers told me not to talk so much. Kids started calling me "Two-Ton Torry," which was cruel, although it was somewhat clever. I laughed with them, yet inside I was crying. It bothered me and made me hide even more. I spoke less and tried to blend in. I even tried to be less smart. My natural tendency to shine was still there, and I reined it in. It was confusing. I wanted to be visible, to be the center of attention, to put myself out there, to be the real me. And I kept hearing messages that told me to be quiet, don't be so visible, don't talk so much, blend in.

This practice continued for most of my life. I vacillated between letting go and being the person who loved being visible, and listening to others who told me to keep quiet, blend in, be like everyone else. It continued through high school, college, grad school, and every job I had. Occasionally I would get to a place where I was comfortable and allow myself to be me—to be the bubbly, vivacious person I was meant to be, to stand out. At those times, I was the happiest, and I loved life. Then someone said or did something, and I went back inside that shell again. It could be a professor, a boss, a boyfriend, or a coworker. I wasn't confident enough to be the me I was born to be against other people's judgments—or sometimes even their perceived judgments. I cared what other people thought. I'm pretty sure my insecurity had me putting thoughts and words into people's heads that were never really there.

For almost sixty years, I went through life this way, bouncing back and forth between my true self and the person I felt others wanted me to be. I would express myself, be visible, be the person I was born to be. Then something would happen, and I would go back to being someone else, less visible, less likely to shine, hiding myself.

Until recently.

A few years ago, I was fired from my job in a horrendous fashion. I drove four hours to a two-day sales meeting, and when I got to the hotel, my room had been canceled. My boss had HR on the phone, and I was told I was being fired and would be paid until the end of the day. Did I mention that I had been with this company for eleven years and was a top performer? That I had just signed the company's largest client, and we were on a call with them that morning? Apparently, I was too visible. My opinions, my values, and where I felt our team should focus differed from my boss, and that was not acceptable. I was being made an example of. If they could fire Lori, then no one was safe.

I was angry, terrified, and embarrassed. I didn't know if I wanted to cry, hit someone, or throw up. How could they do this to me? Why was I being treated so disrespectfully? Why did they make me drive four hours and then fire me? I mean, who does that?

As I started the four-hour drive home, I was a mess. I had to call my husband and tell him what happened. My son was in college, and I had to give him the bad news. Would we be able to pay for his college?

FROM DIMMED TO DAZZLING

How would we pay the bills? What were my co-workers going to think when I wasn't at the meeting after they saw me at the hotel? It was hard to keep my focus on the road.

Suddenly a thought popped into my head. *I DON'T HAVE TO GO TO WORK TOMORROW!* I felt lighter, free, joyful. *I DON'T HAVE TO GO TO WORK TOMORROW! I'M FREE!* I realized I didn't have to work at a job that wouldn't allow me to be the real me. While I liked my job and my customers, I wasn't really happy or fulfilled. No longer did I have to be the person others wanted me to be. I had control. I had a choice. I could do what I wanted to do, and I could be who I was meant to be.

On that drive home, I made the decision to change my life. I didn't know what I would do, and I knew I would never again put my happiness in someone else's hands. I would be in control of my life, and I would live it the way I was meant to live it. That meant I could be visible—I could stand out, be silly, bubbly, loud, passionate, even angry. My life could be lived on my terms. I found my joy, my shine.

Writing a book was something I had always wanted to do and never had the time. So I wrote *The Reinvention Mindset*, and in it I shared my stories, my vulnerabilities and my need to stand out, to be visible, to be famous. And it felt amazing! I wasn't embarrassed anymore. I wasn't hiding. I didn't care what anyone else thought. Being my authentic self was so empowering. Everyone needs to experience this amazing feeling. Everyone needs to know that they, too, have this power, this choice; they can be their authentic self and live in joy.

It didn't stop there. Speaking had always been something I loved, so I became a speaker. I entered speaking competitions, and even won one. Numerous applications were submitted for TEDx events, and I was finally accepted to give a TEDx Talk. I enrolled in speaker training programs. I shared my story, my mission, and my message from the stage. I signed up to be a podcast guest, spoke at conferences, church groups, summits, anywhere I could. Being visible allowed me to encourage others to find their true self, to make a choice to live the life they desire. I was having so much fun.

My beliefs, my vision, and my mission became clear. Life is meant to be lived, one crazy adventure at a time. The world is a joyful place, full of possibilities. Everyone deserves to live the life they desire, to be true to their authentic self. My vision is a world where all people are free to be their authentic self, and my mission is to help as many people as possible achieve this vision.

To do this, I knew I needed to learn more. And learning was one of my core values—it is part of my authentic self—so I loved this. Understanding how the brain worked would be valuable. Learning about the conscious and unconscious mind and why we limit ourselves was necessary. The more I learned and grew, the more I could help others find the joy I had found. I took coaching classes and became a certified life and mindset coach. I learned multiple coaching modalities. I became a certified hypnotherapist. I wanted to learn as much as possible so I could use what I learned to help others. And I had to get out there and share this message.

Being visible is part of my authentic self, and when I embraced this, my life became so much more. I reinvented myself, and now I jump out of bed every morning excited to start the new day.

Visibility might be part of your authentic self, too, and if it is, embrace it, get out there and be seen; let your light shine. We all have a light, and we need to let this light shine. Maybe it's by speaking, by being visible. Yet that's not the only way to let your light shine. Maybe it's teaching, R&D, service, cooking, being a parent, a child, a friend. It doesn't matter what it is. What matters is that it is yours, it makes you joyful and fulfilled, and it lets you shine.

Don't ever dim your light because of what someone else says or thinks. Be true to your authentic self; explore it and embrace it. We all have a vision, a mission, and a message we can share with the world, and when we embrace our true self, when we become who we were meant to be, we will shine. You deserve to dazzle.

Lori McDowell, PhD, is CEO of Reimagine U Strategies and author of *The Reinvention Mindset*. Love and joy are cornerstones of Lori's business. She is a mindset coach, helping high-achieving women find joy and fulfillment in business and life. Lori believes we live our purpose when we embrace our authentic self.

reimagineu.net

FIVE STEPS TO RELIEF FROM OVERWHELM

Cecil McIntosh

Would you like to slow down, relax and smile more often?
Would you like to take breaks more often?
Would you like to stop getting upset over niggling stuff?

You're in the right place. Have an open mind and suspend any judgment until after you have my five steps to relief from overwhelm.

But before I get into the meat of the chapter, let me introduce myself. I immigrated to Canada from Barbados at age twenty, where I had been raised by my grandma and the village.

After graduating from Ryerson University, I began my career in sales. I was always hustling, working day and night to outperform my peers.

And then I had two major significant catastrophes in my life: I experienced divorce and bankruptcy in the same week!

These two events set me on a quest to find clarity and see problems through new eyes.

I heard a voice say, "Open your home and teach what you know."

I followed this guidance and for more than three decades, I have since helped countless people get off the hustle/hamster wheel and be in their flow state, at peace and free of worry.

As entrepreneurs, we're told we have to hustle to make the money, but we're never encouraged to stop and slow down. This leads to overwhelm. Some symptoms include:

- You feel tired, restless, and drained.

76   FIVE STEPS TO RELIEF FROM OVERWHELM

- Forty percent of the week you find yourself swallowing your thoughts in an attempt to fit in and be comfortable.
- You feel a tightness in your throat at least once a week.
- You experience difficulty breathing.
- Your stomach is upset.
- Often when you move, you're in physical pain.

The Five Steps

1. **Identify your enemy.** Let me give you an example. Imagine you're at the airport. You're standing at the check-in desk. In your left hand is your passport and right beside you on your right is your suitcase. The pleasant attendant greets you with a smile, checks your travel documents, stamps them, and wishes you an enjoyable flight.

After waiting for a while, it's time to board the plane. You show your passport and travel documents, and the attendant grins and sends you on your way.

You board the plane are welcomed with an even bigger smile, and the hostess tells you where you can find your seat. To your surprise, she informs you that you are traveling first class. The seats are roomy with lots of leg space, and the atmosphere is seductive. And you have a window seat!

The flight attendant instructs you to fasten your seat belt. Next you are aware of the movement of the plane. You can feel the lifting of the plane as it goes up and then levels off.

You unbuckle your seat belt and the flight attendant comes by with drinks. Oh, how time seems to fly, when you're basking in enjoyment and being served. Before you know it, it's time to buckle your seat belt again as the plane begins its descent.

From your window seat as you descend you notice a small land mass, which seems to get larger the closer you get to it. You notice the water, the boats, and the brilliant coastline, and you enjoy another moment of bliss.

Next, you feel a touch as though the wheel of the plane has kissed the earth. There's loud applause. The plane comes to a stop and you're allowed to remove your seat belt. You gather you hand luggage and prepare to leave the plane. The journey through customs is a breeze, and the wait to fetch your luggage is short.

FIVE STEPS TO RELIEF FROM OVERWHELM

After your exit from the airport, you are greeted by a sign with your name on it. An attendant takes your luggage and asks you what three things you would like to do after you check in at your hotel.

First, you're taken to your hotel and given you keys to your room. When you get to your room, you notice that on the bed is a swimsuit, just your size, with a throw to wear over it, slippers, and a hat.

Then you're taken to the three places you requested.

I am going to leave you for a moment to enjoy your three stops.

Now it's time to return to your hotel, change your clothes, and be taken back to the airport.

You board the plane, enjoy the pampering in first class, and the next thing you know, you are right back where you started.

As you were reading this, what was your experience?

You might no longer have tension in your neck or shoulder; you're not clenching your teeth either. You feel as light as a feather.

But what if you did not feel any different?

This was an opportunity to see how uptight you are, but you might not have been aware of this. Now you are.

2. **Journal about your thoughts and feelings.** Keeping a journal helps you to become consciously aware of the patterns of behavior that are creating havoc in your life. You'll have evidence that *you are the problem.* With this new understanding, you can ask questions that will give you more clarity because you have proof of what's happening. If you journal every day for ten days, you'll be able to look back and notice the recurring patterns.

Keep in mind that it's important to have compassion and not beat yourself up. This is an important part of your journey to self-discovery.

3. **Control your thoughts.** I have a client with whom I worked for over six years. She had an awesome program that would have had a great impact on the world. But she ended up with a stroke on her left side. When we got to the root of the issue, she acknowledged that she had a belief that she had to serve others first. So, she neglected her self-care.

NOTE: A belief is something that you accept without evidence.

Belief: Serving others first makes you happy and more money.

No evidence: Does everyone think like this or is it only you?

Belief: Serving others makes you happy and more money.

No evidence: Have you considered that if you serve others first and it doesn't work out, it's not wasted time?

Belief: Serving others first makes you happy and more money.

No evidence: Does that mean you will be able to pay your rent or you'll end up as a bag lady?

4. Slow down. One of the biggest challenges with entrepreneurs is impatience and wanting to force life to go faster.

In life there's a lot of noise. Your phone, people chattering, television, etc. These are all external, but the noise that's most deadly is your inner chatter. You ignore it, try to push it away or have a drink. The dilemma is it does not go away; instead, it takes you down the rabbit hole, and you get stuck down there because it never stops. And you keep on chasing.

That's what I refer to as running the red light. If you did that when driving your car, you'll create all kinds of havoc. Plus, you're breaking the law. However, when you run the red light in your mind, no one supervises you. But you *don't get away with it*, because you're tried, exhausted, and drained by days' end.

The problem is your inner chatter. Here's an exercise to fix that problem.

See yourself driving along. You see a stoplight coming up. As it turns yellow, you prepare to stop so your car stops right before the white line.

Repeat this exercise three times or as much as is necessary to stop your inner chatter.

5. Practice self-reflection. On a scale of 1 to 10, identify where you are, with 1 being relaxed and worry-free and 10 being in full overwhelm. Look back over your journal, paying attention to your awareness, recurring patterns, beliefs, and running the red light. Learn to monitor your awareness, habits, mindset, and pace through life. Check in with yourself every ten days or so.

Then get ready to experience incredible growth and peace.

Have fun!

Cecil McIntosh is a relaxation expert, spiritual teacher, and author. After experiencing two major catastrophes in the same week—divorce and bankruptcy—he now works with successful life coaches to transform their overwhelming workloads into streamlined, impactful coaching practices.

cecilmcintosh.com

INTEGRITY, HONESTY, VISIBILITY

Dr. Sree Meleth

I had run out of money. I had invested in three separate programs: Suzanne Evans' Spotlight, Dannella Burnett's SNTS Inner Circle, and the Seven-Figure Podcasting Program. I had resigned from my 175k job in February, and by August, I was out of savings and the business was not yet generating the income I needed. My credit cards were maxed out, and I could no longer use them.

I had a two thousand dollar pension and another two thousand dollars from Social Security. I had secretly taken some money from our joint savings account, and now I was "stealing" checks from our joint checking account to fund me.

I am a transformational life coach who uses Emotional Freedom Technique (EFT), meditation, and visualizations to help my clients overcome subconscious stories that are keeping them from achieving their full potential. I am very good at what I do. Testimonials like this one are common:

> *One session with Dr. Sree, and I couldn't believe that something I'd been struggling with my whole life had completely changed.*
> —Kristine Skiff, Gift an Author Publishing

Yet money was not flowing in. Clients who provided glowing testimonials after a session failed to book the remaining sessions. Many sales calls ended with "I want to work with you, but I don't have the money."

I promised myself that I knew exactly how much I had "borrowed" from my husband and that once my business turned the corner, I would start paying him back with 20 percent interest. I justified my secrecy with this silent promise.

Being dishonest did not feel good. I wished I could talk honestly with my husband. I would think to myself, *I wish our relationship was different; I wish he was more supportive.* Subtly I was making it his fault that I was behaving without integrity.

This was not the only place in my personal life I was dishonest. I wasn't honest with my daughter either. I pretended everything was fine and dandy when it wasn't. I remembered a conversation I had with my son, almost thirteen years ago, almost two years after I had moved out and was struggling with what I wanted to do next.

"You are pushing away all the people who are here to support you," he had said.

It was true. In the entire two years that I stayed out of our marriage, my husband had not once given up us. He was steadfast in his commitment. The following paragraphs are from my book *More Than Peace, Power & Presence through Meditation.*

Even when I was a young eight- or ten-year-old, I knew that I wanted to do something big, that I wanted to be written about and interviewed. There was a knowing deep down that I was meant to experience all that. But then life interfered. My mother died in a plane crash when I was nineteen. I suddenly became responsible for a household with two older brothers—one who was struggling with the throes of an early marriage and the other who was rapidly descending into alcoholism.

I tried to escape that responsibility by agreeing to an arranged marriage. I became a mother ten months after I got married and ended up right back in Bombay with my birth family while my husband tried to relocate to the Middle East. Once he relocated, we moved more than twenty-five times across three continents while raising two kids.

Nearly thirty years later, the stress of a high-powered job, the impact it had on my marriage, and my father's death all resulted in me deciding I needed time off from my responsibilities as a wife. I felt like I had not taken a full breath since the night my mother's plane crashed and turned my world upside down. It is an overused phrase, I know, but I really needed to find myself.

That search took me a good two-and-a-half years. I believe I did find myself and am becoming better and better at articulating for myself what I want and asking for it without fear or the emotional manipulation that fear of openly asking for my needs often resulted in.

Yet here I was, back to the place where fear and emotional manipulation were being used because of the terror I felt at openly asking for what I needed. I was in a different place, our marriage was in a completely different, much healthier place, but it was so much easier to fall into an old pattern.

This was not a comfortable place to be in. I began using my own techniques on myself. I meditated; I prayed; I tapped. The first glimmer of light was when the words *he is not an adversary; he is your support system* came to me as I tapped. As the days went by and I continued praying, tapping, and meditating, the next transformation was acknowledging that I deserved to be supported, that I was an amazing human being with the potential to help thousands, and I deserved to invest in myself.

As these messages settled inside me, my sales conversations changed. More people signed up to be coached by me. A few even paid in full for my VIP Dream Sessions. The energy around my business was changing.

I was still not there, though. The business was growing, and I was being more visible. Everywhere I spoke, I blew people away with my authenticity and grace. However, there was still a block. As I mentioned before, despite amazing experiences in their sessions, clients were experiencing blocks in their money flow, resulting in them waiting to pay me. I had not yet set up a system for auto-pays, so my business was dependent on them keeping their word. Several clients who had promised to sign up in August were now backing away.

A few days ago, I started using Dr. Joe Dispensa's meditations. As I tune into the infinite potentials in the quantum field, he asks the question: "Who do you want to be? How does the person who is abundant or has achieved what you are trying to manifest behave? What are the characteristics?"

"She has integrity, she is transparent, and she is unafraid to be visible with all of her imperfections." As these words rang out in my mind, I felt my heart open, I felt my throat open, and I also felt terrified. I knew that the time of hiding had ended. My business could only thrive if I was willing to be honest, transparent, and visible in my personal life. It was not possible to be dishonest, manipulative, and fearful in one part of life and be in integrity in my business.

I finally did it. I sat down last night and told my husband I needed help. I told him that I had used checks from our joint account and deposited them into my account. I also told him of the possibilities that were opening up in Freeing Ourselves. I explained that I had a high-ticket offer that I had validated. I told him that I believed I was on the verge of turning things around. I had a record of the money I had borrowed, and I promised I would pay it back.

There were no fireworks. My house did not crash around me. We continued to communicate like two adults. I had reached a place where I was comfortable asking for support, settled in the knowledge that I deserved that support.

I cannot yet report that my business has suddenly blossomed and is now a seven-figure business, but I know that its foundations are solid. I know that once again I am true to the name of my business, Freeing Ourselves, and I know that can and must lead to great things.

A transformational life coach, certified EFT practitioner, and public health researcher, **Dr. Sree Meleth** founded Freeing Ourselves to help clients overcome self-doubt and step into their highest potential. Sree gently holds space for her clients to work through their distress and come out on the other side with a calm, powerful belief in themselves.

freeingourselves.com

ARE YOU TOO SMART FOR YOUR OWN SUCCESS?

Nancy Michieli

You can have all the brainpower in the world, but you have to transmit it. Transmission is communication.
—*Warren Buffet*

"Breathe, Nancy." As the words came over the phone, I was puzzled.

"Breathe, what do you mean? I am breathing," I retorted.

"Not for you, Nancy, for me," my boss said. "I need you to breathe so I have time to process everything you've said."

You see, I had spent the last twenty minutes on an excited, empathic rant about why his choice of software was "a stupid waste of money" and how he already had the solution without any additional cost.

When I am stressed, very excited, or a combination of both, I tend to overcommunicate. I desperately want to get my point across, so I speak lots of excess words, take very few breaths, and go on and on until I feel completely satisfied.

See how I just did that? *Completely* is an excess word.

It's part of my nature to try to be perfect, to share perfectly, and to ensure I have not missed a point. But the problem with trying to communicate perfectly is that it can negatively affect your credibility.

At that moment, my boss was kind as he gave me the feedback to breathe and pause. I often see this same pattern in many brilliant engineers and logically minded people: a need to be perfect and overcommunicate.

Recently, as I was working with a technical team, an engineer—let's call him George—started to speak in a meeting. He quickly got on his high horse about some topic and repeatedly said the same thing over and over as he tried to make his point perfectly.

Even though everyone was in a Zoom meeting with cameras off, I knew they were all rolling their eyes, shaking their heads, or checking out, thinking, *Here he goes again.* They were hoping and praying for him to just stop talking.

Later that day, when I went to book a technical discussion requiring George's participation, they all asked how it could happen without George.

George had ruined his credibility. It didn't matter how brilliant George was; because he couldn't speak well, people didn't want to work with him, impacting his success.

So, if communicating with perfection reduces credibility, then what makes someone come across as brilliant? Yes, they need their knowledge or skills, but that is not what makes them brilliant. What makes them brilliant in our eyes is their ability to take complex ideas and distill them down to the simplest form.

It's like the old saying, "If you can't explain it simply, you don't understand it well enough." While Einstein didn't say it (and we don't know who did), this philosophy will serve you well.

More than ever, our bright-minded, technical, geeky people can gain more influence and buy-in to their ideas the better they get at communicating them simply.

Let's take a moment to consider Steve Jobs, one of the most powerful and impactful technical speakers we have ever heard.

His speaking attributes consist of the following:

1. He focused on one idea at a time.
2. His PowerPoint slides were pictures or a few words.
3. He avoided using techie jargon.
4. He connected on a human level about needs, not features and specifications.
5. He had a confident, relaxed demeanor.

ARE YOU TOO SMART FOR YOUR OWN SUCCESS? 89

6. He used powerful pauses.
7. He practiced speaking.

How can you apply "the Steve Jobs effect" to make you more credible and successful in your career? Implement these seven attributes into your corporate speaking:

1. **Focus on one idea at a time.** Before speaking, consider the one thing you want someone to feel, think differently about, or take action on. Too often, as technical people, we want to share too much, so we lose impact. But instead reflect before speaking on the point you want to land by "starting with the end in mind." You'll have a significantly better chance to motivate someone to think differently, feel differently, or take action.

2. **Learn Powerpoint simplicity:** I could write a whole chapter on PowerPoint in business, but here is the key: On each slide, use a maximum of one sentence, short and to the point, or a photo. Engineers love to put way too much information on one slide. The PowerPoint presentation is intended to support your point; the best way to do this is visually, allowing the words to come from your lips.

3. **Avoid techie jargon and acronyms.** I have sat in too many meetings and presentations when people used techie jargon and acronyms, causing confusion instead of clarity. This is a key sign you are trying to *sound* smart instead of *being* smart. I recommend watching Steve Jobs's launch presentation of the iPad. He could take complex topics and distill them into everyday language connected to the people with whom he was sharing. Remember, only some people in the room, even technical people, will have the same knowledge base. Still, the better you use everyday language, the more successful it will be, making you sound more intelligent and capable.

4. **Connect on a human-to-human level.** If you want people to listen to you, start with remembering "What's in it for them?" When you communicate with the receiver in mind, it adjusts how you

speak and makes your hearers feel valued and respected. In Steve Jobs's launch of the iPad, he didn't talk about features; he shared statements like "You can hold the internet in your hands," "You can manipulate with your fingers," and "It's the best experience you've ever had." When you put the other person's experience front and center in your communication, you'll have them in the palm of your hand.

5. **Have a confident, relaxed demeanor.** When you speak, do you express a confident, relaxed demeanor? You can tell by your breathing—whether it is shallow, quick, slow, or relaxed. Your body language should be relaxed shoulders and jaw, no gritting of the teeth. Your posture is confident. When people see a calm, confident speaker, their body language naturally adjusts to the speaker. This is known as mirroring. It increases likability and builds trust. But speaking with tension in your jaw or shoulder can cause the same tension in those listening, causing distrust. So, before you talk, take time to check your body. Is it confident and relaxed? If not, take deep, slow breaths to recenter yourself and then speak.

6. **Understand the power of the pause:** Steve Jobs was a master at the power of the pause. Pausing using your breath gives time for your idea to land, sink in, and get an emotional response. When you watch videos of Steve Jobs, you'll notice that he pauses often and for a few seconds. The impact is powerful. As someone still working to develop this skill and release the need to fill the dead air, I use this time to breathe. Taking a breath allows me to relax my body so I continue to show up with confidence. I also observe the reactions of others. Can I visually see the response to what I am saying? Is it getting the reaction I expect or do they look confused? The ability to pause gives whomever you are speaking with time to catch up, time to build trust, and time to relax with you.

7. **Practice your communication:** The final thing top leaders do to earn more credibility is to practice communicating. You may think, *I don't need to practice; I've been communicating my entire life.* However, I challenge you to consider that you have been *talking* your entire life, which is not the same as communicating. Talking

can be without intention. It is often just me-focused and lacks connection. Communicating, on the other hand, is focused on the receiver. It requires thought, inquiry, and the ability to see, hear, and observe how what you're communicating is landing. The best communicators in the world practice becoming incredible speakers. They rehearse their ideas to make them simple, clear, and focused. They think about stories or metaphors that illustrate their point. They keep the person they want to impact uppermost in mind. They ask for feedback on how they can improve.

If you want to be respected for your brilliance, and if you want to become more successful, then you must become an exceptional communicator.

Consider the amount of time you have invested in becoming brilliant in your area of knowledge or skill. Now, take that same effort and invest it in your ability to communicate your area of expertise with simplicity. It will pay dividends.

As Plato said, "A wise man speaks because he has something to say, a fool speaks because he has to say something."

This is your opportunity to shine, be successful, and be the most respected person in your area of expertise. Don't let it pass you by because you can't speak well.

Nancy Michieli saved an unheard of $9 million in nine months leading turnarounds in the petrochemical industry. As a speaker, hypnotist, executive leadership coach, and sommelier with decades in engineering leadership, she now helps engineers and logically minded people communicate and collaborate to achieve impossible results.

nancymichielicoaching.com

VISIBILITY IN ACTION: BE SEEN, BE HEARD, BE THE CHANGE, LEAD THE CHANGE

Drocella Mugorewera

Introduction

What do you do when your voice and visibility is taken away? How do you recover from the trauma of being betrayed by people you trusted?

It was hard to recover my visibility activities after being silenced and cut off from my family and the world when I was forced to flee my country, Rwanda, as a refugee in 2008. I remember like it was yesterday when I had to go out late in the middle of the night for fresh air when other people were sleeping so nobody would notice me. As a former member of parliament and a public figure who had appeared on TV and radio, delivering public speeches in front of local, regional, and international audiences, it was very challenging for me to hide and be quiet—especially when I saw injustice, and problems I could solve.

Visibility has been an integral part of my integration in America. Visibility helped to rebuild my confidence. In 2015, my future self questioned me about how long I was going to continue to hide. I then applied for the Executive Director (ED) of Bridge Refugee Services, the agency that welcomed me in Knoxville, Tennessee, in 2009.

After serving as ED for six-and-a-half years, I heard a call to go bigger and work with police departments and minority groups. I started to network like a Ninja. After faith, networking is my second superpower. One day I heard brand catalyst mentor Sammy Garrity speaking at an event, and I was attracted to talk to her. I told her what I wanted to do, and she helped me to work on my vision of building the Diversity IN Action Global Movement, which helps corporate decision makers eliminate employee turnover and save money on hiring and rehiring by turning employees into loyal ambassadors of their brands. The solution to employee retention is building relationships and trust among teams.

Regaining Confidence through Visibility

I had to use my resilience muscles to shift, step into the spotlight, share ideas, and speak on issues related to my experience of being different. Regaining public exposure helped me not only to share my message but also to refine and elevate it. I learned how to tell my story, and now I invite companies that collaborate with me to embed storytelling in their company culture.

Now I present my Diversity IN Action Framework to a global audience with confidence, showing leaders new ways of dealing with employee retention and attraction challenges.

In embracing diversity and fostering inclusion, we not only enrich our communities and workplaces but also ignite a beacon of hope for a world where every voice is heard, every perspective valued, and every individual empowered to thrive. —Drocella Mugorewera

Key Takeaway: Confidence is built through exposure and practice. The more visible you are, the more empowered you feel to articulate your vision and drive impact. Visibility helps to spread your message and driving systemic change.

Becoming a Number-One Bestselling Author through Visibility

Growing my visibility gave me the opportunity to share my story on different platforms, including podcasts. The connection with Payman Lorenzo, the podcast host of *Leaders With A Heart*, will always be memorable because it led to being a contributing author in the book *Leaders With A Heart Volume I: Global Entrepreneurs Creating Massive Impact*.

Bernice Williams also invited me to be a contributing author to the book *With Grace and Grit: Inspirational Guideposts for Women in Business*. These books enabled me to reach even more people and share my insights and thoughts on topics I care about, such as refugee and immigrant integration. Additionally, networking, both online and in person, has expanded my circle of influence, allowing for new connections with thought leaders, entrepreneurs, and visionaries around the globe.

Through visibility, I was invited by Dr. L, The Parent Whisperer, to contribute to *The Parenting Owner's Manual*, where I wrote about the role of families in promoting language diversity and equity. I believe that in the current global economy, working in one language is no longer sufficient. Producing empathetic leaders starts at an early age. I recommend giving your child the gift of learning another language and master it for life and service.

Key Takeaway: Visibility opens doors not only for personal achievements, like authoring a book, but also for growing an influential network.

Winning through Visibility: Stepping into the Spotlight Transformed My Speaking Journey

In October 2023, I had the opportunity to attend the Visibility Event hosted by Dannella Burnett in Atlanta, Georgia. I participated in the speakers' competition. To my delight, I secured third place, winning a total prize package worth $28,881, which included five hundred dollars in cash.

Key Takeaway: Visibility is not just about being seen but also about creating tangible results—whether it is delivering your message with clarity and conviction or accessing resources that accelerate your goals.

Unlocking Speaking and Consulting Opportunities

Visibility led to speaking engagements across multiple platforms and stages. Through visibility, I also secured business contracts. Here is what Nao Kabashima, executive director of Karen Organization of San Diego (KOSD) says:

KOSD started to work with Drocella in 2023. Drocella is an inspiring woman leader and mentor helping us to be a compassionate, ethical, and sustainable ethnic community-based organization for our community. As a consultant, she is reliable and always thrives to co-direct us to carry out our own mission and values, not dictating our decisions. She says, "Our voices, ideas, perspectives, backgrounds, skills, talents, experiences, and cultures matter. Inclusion practices are non-negotiable," and this quote exactly shows who she is and how she works with and supports others.

Key Takeaway: Speaking opportunities foster credibility and open avenues for impactful collaborations.

Learning New Tools: The Power of AI and Business Growth

Visibility exposes me to new tools, particularly the integration of AI in business, which I may not have encountered otherwise. Through visibility I met Thomas Gay, founder of Chat Bridge and EngagePro. These tools have empowered me to manage my time more efficiently and ultimately focus on scaling my Diversity IN Action Global Movement. Being visible allows me to keep learning, evolving, and staying ahead of the curve.

Key Takeaway: Visibility leads to exposure to the latest tools and techniques, helping you stay competitive in an ever-changing world.

The Power of Gratitude and Repetition

Through visibility, I've had mastermind sessions with different experts. We read books together and were assigned accountability partners. I learned the power of writing things down and speaking them aloud. Practicing gratitude and repetition helped me to stay motivated and focus on activities that serve my goals.

Key Takeaway: Gratitude and consistency build a foundation for long-lasting visibility and success.

A Renewed Morning Routine and Accountability Partners

Visibility inspired me to establish a morning routine focused on physical and mental well-being, including daily workouts, drinking water, and power hours. This routine has helped me maintain balance and productivity. Having accountability partners helps keep me on track, celebrating wins, and supporting me in challenges.

Key Takeaway: Consistency, a supportive network, and personal wellness plan are critical for sustaining visibility and leadership.

Hosting the First Summit: A Milestone in Visibility

Visibility led to hosting my first Virtual Employee Retention Revolution Summit, featuring sixteen speakers with whom I connected through in-person and online events. I am grateful for Dannella Burnett and her team's technical assistance. This summit was a culmination of my visibility journey, showcasing my ability to lead, collaborate, and create impactful platforms for diverse voices. What I learned during this process is to be calm, trust the process, and communicate effectively.

Key Takeaway: Hosting a summit is a powerful testament to the value of visibility in building networks and leading collaborative initiatives.

Increasing Your Social Media Presence

Visibility transformed my social media presence, particularly on LinkedIn. Visibility on social media has connected me with new opportunities, expanded my influence, and brought greater awareness to the Diversity IN Action movement and Framework.

Key Takeaway: Social media is a key tool for increasing visibility, connecting with audiences, and amplifying your mission.

The Power of Visibility and the Road Ahead

Visibility has transformed my life, business, and the diversity global movement I am building. Visibility is not just about being seen but about making meaningful connections, sharing your vision, and driving impactful change.

I encourage the readers to embrace visibility as a tool for personal and professional growth. I am grateful for everyone who contributed to the reviving of my leadership resilience and my growth.

If your company is struggling with employee turnover, seek help from experts in the field. We are here to help.

Drocella Mugorewera, founder of the Diversity IN Action Global Movement, helps employers stop the costly cycle of hiring and rehiring. She empowers companies to eliminate turnover, save money, and create loyal brand ambassadors. Her proven strategies build sustainable workplaces where employees thrive, driving long-term success and retention.

drocella.com

TAKE CHARGE OF YOUR HEALTHCARE: THREE ROADBLOCKS TO OVERCOME FOR SAFER CARE!

Cathy S. Otten, RN, BSN

One sentence changed my entire opinion of my career in healthcare. "Whew, we almost lost him in there," said the doctor. We had been waiting for two hours past the time we were told my father would be finished with his "simple procedure" and were growing concerned. The doctor said he had an unexpected event that was now under control, but my dad wouldn't be discharged for another four to six hours. Without any further explanation, the doctor left the consult room.

Honestly, I think I blacked out for a second, I was so shocked. After coming to my senses, I requested a social worker to come talk to my mom and me. She was able to get some of the answers we needed. Evidently Dad had excessive bleeding at the end of the procedure; they didn't know why but wanted to observe him before discharging him. I asked her to help me complete the paperwork—copies of the referral notes from his primary care physician and any other physician, the surgeon's history and physical, pre-op, lab work, and the operative procedure note when completed. The social worker was a godsend, and we left with most of the paperwork in hand. After two weeks, I had everything I needed. However, I found that his medical and surgical histories were incomplete and contained errors, his medication list was disturbingly wrong, his list of providers was incomplete, and none of his providers over three different healthcare systems matched. As a registered nurse for more than thirty-five years, I was devastated, angry—and now on a mission: I was going to empower patients and their families to learn how to navigate the roadblocks in the healthcare system.

Here are strategies to overcome three major roadblocks along the way to enjoy safer healthcare, healthier outcomes, and possibly lessen your medical expenses.

Roadblock Number One

The Electronic Medical (Health) Record (EMR/EHR) has changed the way we gather, record, and disseminate patient information. The intention was to be able to provide seamless sharing of information. The problems are that humans enter the information, and different healthcare systems have separate EMR/EHRs that don't share with one another. Unless a problem is found, there is no audit of information entered. This means the wrong information is used and shared until there is a problem.

Steps to Audit and Correct Your EMR/HER: The first step is to complete a Request for Information (ROI) form; this may take thirty to ninety days to receive. Some systems may charge you a per-page fee. This step will take the longest to complete and will be the most difficult. Take small steps and don't become discouraged.

1. Request a copy of your medical, surgical, gyn (if appropriate), family, social, medication, and allergy histories.
2. Request a copy of your last visit note from each doctor with whom you are currently following up.
3. Request a copy of the discharge note from the last hospitalization, emergency room visit, or urgent care visit. These notes should include laboratory and biopsy results and radiology reports.
4. While waiting on the above, start documenting your own record of the information in step number one. Be sure to use correct terminology and spelling as much as possible. Include dates and doctor/hospital, if known for each entry. Be sure to include important childhood history that may be affecting your current health.

When you receive your all the requested information and complete your written history, you can then start to compare the information.

Fill in the gaps in your written history and correct any incorrect information in the providers' histories. Be sure to mark the errors that are in the EMR/EHR. Next, request that the records to be corrected. Depending on the system you may have to go through some hoops to accomplish this. However, in the end, you will be satisfied that the information is correct. Stay calm and try not to get emotional or angry when going through the process. I did have to get a lawyer to send a letter to one MD to get the correction I requested. That is a last resort, however, and is usually not required. Be persistent in making sure the changes you've requested have been made.

In our case, we found the PCP didn't have a list of the other providers taking care of my dad, so that information wasn't passed on to the surgeon. Also, my mom brought a list of medications she thought important and pertinent to the procedure and the problem he was having treated, but it wasn't complete. Another finding was that the blood thinner medication had been discontinued by the prescribing MD six years earlier, but for an unknown reason, the primary care doctor kept renewing it. YIKES!

Roadblock Number Two—Medication List

This is a part of the medical history, but it's important enough to have a section of its own.

1. Gather all prescription medications and make a list. If you have discontinued medications or expired medications, discard them. It is too easy to accidentally request refills on meds you should not be taking.

2. Include, if known, the date started. Often, when starting a new medication, a provider will schedule you to come in for an appointment to review if desired effect is happening or if you are tolerating the drug. If you have an appointment for a follow-up appointment in two weeks, and the pharmacy gets the medication to you twelve days after it was ordered, you will have only taken it for two days before seeing the doctor. Now you've paid for a visit that was unnecessary and a waste of time and money. Call and reschedule the appointment as soon as you know the start of a new medication will be delayed.

3. Make sure you know who the ordering physician is so you know who to call for refills and any problems.
4. Be aware of the reason it was prescribed as other providers or emergency personnel will often ask why you are taking a certain drug.
5. If possible, list both the brand and generic name of the drug. This was one of the problems with the surgery center and Mom missing the blood thinner. My mom left it off the list, When the nurse specifically asked my mom if my dad was taking a blood thinner and if it was Coumadin, Mom said no because she didn't recognize the brand name (he was taking warfarin, the generic name).
6. Know the size (milligrams) of each pill, the recommended dosage, and any other instructions on the bottle.

At the top of your medication list, list your name or the name of the person to whom the list belongs, along with any allergies and the pharmacy you use. Keep a copy of this list so it's available to take to all your doctor appointments, and be sure to update as needed as soon as a change is made.

Roadblock Three—The Doctor's Visit

Doctors' offices have rules that must be followed when scheduling patient visits. These include the number and type of patients to be seen in a day and how long the time slots are for each type of visit. New patients might get thirty minutes to an hour depending on the practice. Follow-up appointments might be only seven minutes or up to twenty minutes long. Often these appointments are scheduled one after the other with a thirty- to sixty-minute break for lunch. If patients are late for their appointment or a fifteen-minute appointment turns into forty, the wait time for everyone is extended. A patient emergency in the office that requires an ambulance or emergency phone calls from the hospital or other doctors caring for mutual patients are the most common reasons. What can you do to not be the cause of the traffic jam?

Know the reason for the appointment.

1. Be ready to discuss any problems related to the reason for the visit.
2. If you have questions or problems unrelated to the visit, consider rescheduling or call the office and request extra time.

TAKE CHARGE OF YOUR HEALTHCARE

3. Be prepared, with your questions written down, and don't hesitate to speak up during the appointment.
4. Don't forget to bring the medications list with you to the appointment.

As you encounter these three potential roadblocks and are prepared to deal with them, you will begin to see a difference in how you and your doctor interact with each other. You will leave each appointment feeling seen and heard, and you will be clear about what your next steps are going forward. You will have the healthcare information in your hand when you face an unexpected crisis, and you will be confident it is correct. There is much more you can do to be an active participant in your healthcare in order to feel prepared and empowered.

Cathy S. Otten RN, BSN, leveraging her thirty-five years as a registered nurse, offers her expertise as your go-to healthcare coach. Cathy ensures that you no longer leave your doctor's appointments feeling confused or unheard. Cathy's goal is to help you evolve from a simple patient to an active participant in your healthcare journey.

healthcareconsumertraining.com

IS YOUR WEIGHT KEEPING YOU INVISIBLE?

ANN ROLLE

Have you ever walked into a room and felt like no one noticed you? Like your voice was drowned out by the noise of societal expectations—or worse, ignored altogether? This feeling of invisibility isn't just a fleeting thought; it's a reality that many women grapple with daily.

"Is that what a woman needs to do . . . just lose weight to get attention?" These poignant words from Rebel Wilson, a Hollywood actress named one of the BBC's 100 Women of 2021, echo a sentiment felt by countless women around the world. Rebel knows what it's like to feel invisible—not because of a lack of talent or intelligence, but because society often equates worth with appearance.

For many who struggle with excess weight, the feelings of invisibility are deeply rooted in societal pressures, personal challenges, and the overwhelming demands of their professional and personal lives. It's not just about physical health; it's about being seen, heard, and valued in a world that often overlooks those who don't fit into a narrow mold of beauty.

Too many women silently carry the weight of invisibility alone, feeling as though they must fight an uphill battle just to be noticed. But what if the key to releasing this invisible weight lies not in fitting into a societal mold, but in embracing a personalized approach to health and nutrition that celebrates your uniqueness?

As a holistic nutritionist and weight loss coach, I've seen firsthand the profound effects of excess weight on the body, mind, and emotions.

The Invisible Weight: Understanding the Impact

Societal Bias and Media Portrayals

Society's standards of beauty are often narrow, rigid, and unforgiving, especially toward women. Media portrayals contribute significantly to the feeling of invisibility for overweight women by consistently promoting an idealized image of thinness as the standard of beauty and success. This pervasive narrative pushes those who do not fit into this mold into the background, making them feel unworthy and unseen.

The "invisible weight" these women carry isn't just physical; it's emotional and psychological. It's the burden of living in a world that measures their worth by the number on a scale rather than their character, talents, or contributions. This weight manifests in various aspects of life:

- **Workplace:** Research by economist David Lempert revealed that overweight women begin their careers with lower wages and receive fewer promotions and raises over time, significantly impacting their cumulative earnings. This disparity is further exacerbated as women climb the corporate ladder, where overweight female executives can face a wage penalty as high as 16 percent.
- **Financial Impact:** A report by the National Institute of Health found that the financial net worth of moderately to severely obese women aged fifty-one to sixty-one is 40 percent lower than that of their normal-weight peers. This financial disparity can affect their quality of life, including their ability to retire comfortably, access healthcare, and achieve financial security.
- **Social Gatherings:** The pressure to conform to certain body images creates feelings of inadequacy, making social interactions challenging. Many women feel judged or inadequate in social settings, leading to social withdrawal and isolation reinforcing the cycle of invisibility.
- **Airline Travel:** Public spaces, such as airlines, are another area where overweight individuals often feel marginalized. For example, the simple act of requesting a seat belt extension can lead to embarrassment or negative reactions from flight attendants, exacerbating feelings of shame and invisibility.

IS YOUR WEIGHT KEEPING YOU INVISIBLE?

- **Healthcare:** In healthcare settings, overweight women may receive less attention or have their health concerns dismissed or attributed solely to their weight. This can lead to missed diagnoses and inadequate care, putting their health at greater risk.

The Emotional, Physical, and Mental Health Impact

Weight Stigma and Its Consequences

Weight stigma is both a social issue and a significant public health concern. It undermines health behaviors and preventive care, leading to disordered eating, decreased physical activity, healthcare avoidance, and ultimately, even more weight gain. The psychological toll of weight stigma contributes to stress, anxiety, depression, and a diminished quality of life. Over time, these factors increase the risk of chronic diseases and even mortality.

Impact on Self-Esteem and Quality of Life

For many women, the constant battle with weight stigma results in a significant blow to their self-esteem and confidence. The relentless pressure to conform to societal standards of beauty can lead to feelings of inadequacy, shame, and guilt. This can manifest in various ways, such as avoiding social interactions, dressing to camouflage their size, or avoiding photos to remain invisible. Over time, this can make it increasingly difficult to pursue personal and professional goals.

Healthcare Avoidance

The stigma associated with being overweight can lead to a decrease in health-seeking behaviors. Many women avoid seeking medical care due to fear of being judged or dismissed by healthcare providers. This avoidance can result in missed or delayed diagnoses, leading to more severe health issues that could have been prevented with timely intervention. The healthcare system's failure to provide equitable care leaves women feeling invisible, unheard, and uncared for.

Impact on Daily Life

Obesity can significantly limit a woman's ability to participate in daily activities. The physical discomfort associated with carrying excess weight, such as joint pain, fatigue, and mobility issues, can make everyday tasks challenging. Additionally, the struggle to find clothing that fits comfortably can be a constant reminder of societal pressures, further diminishing self-esteem. The emotional burden of obesity can lead to social withdrawal, further perpetuating the cycle of invisibility.

Releasing the Weight of Invisibility: Why One-Size-Fits-All Diets Fail

In my profession, I've witnessed the damaging effects of the "one size fits all" approach to dieting. Each of us is unique, with different backgrounds, cultures, lifestyles, and genetic makeups. What works for one person may not work for another, and the pressure to conform to a specific diet can lead to frustration, failure, and a further sense of invisibility.

Customized nutrition offers an alternative—a holistic approach that considers individual physical, mental, and emotional well-being to create personalized nutrition plans tailored to one's biochemistry, genetic makeup, lifestyle, and preferences. This approach acknowledges that there is no one-size-fits-all solution to health and wellness and that true success lies in understanding and embracing your unique needs.

Customized Nutrition: Your Path to Visibility

Personalized Precision
Customized nutrition is about more than just what you eat; it's about how your body processes and utilizes food. By considering factors such as your genetic makeup, metabolic rate, and lifestyle, a customized nutrition plan can provide the precise nutrients your body needs to function optimally. This personalized approach ensures that your body is receiving the right balance of nutrients to support your health goals, whether that's weight loss, improved energy levels, or enhanced mental clarity.

Nourishment, Not Deprivation
Unlike restrictive diets that focus on cutting calories or eliminating entire food groups, customized nutrition emphasizes nourishment. It's about fueling your body with nutrient-dense foods that provide sustained energy, support mental and emotional well-being, and promote overall

vitality. This approach shifts the focus from deprivation to abundance, helping you develop a healthy relationship with food that supports long-term success.

Holistic Harmony

Customized nutrition considers the whole you—every aspect of your life, including your physical, mental, and emotional health. It's about creating a plan that aligns with your lifestyle, preferences, and goals, ensuring that you can maintain healthy habits in the long term. This holistic approach recognizes that true health is about balance and that sustainable success comes from nurturing all aspects of your well-being.

The Power of Support

Embarking on a weight loss journey can be challenging, but you don't have to do it alone. Customized nutrition provides you with a compassionate guide who offers support, encouragement, and direction every step of the way. Whether you're struggling with cravings, facing a plateau, or simply need someone to talk to, having a supportive coach can make all the difference in your journey toward reclaiming your visibility.

Benefits of a Tailored Approach to Weight Loss

- Customized meals that fit seamlessly into your daily life, allowing you to enjoy food without stress or guilt
- Meals designed specifically for your unique genetic makeup, ensuring that your body receives the nutrients it needs to thrive
- Sustained weight loss, increased energy, and renewed confidence, allowing you to fully participate in life
- Enhanced well-being, including improved mood, mental clarity, and overall vitality, so you can live your best life

Reclaim Your Presence: The Power of Visibility

Remember, your value is not determined by your weight or appearance. Embrace your self-worth, talents, accomplishments, and contributions, especially in the workplace. Prioritize self-care, connect with others who share similar experiences, and shift your internal dialogue to focus on positivity and hope.

Address the challenges of invisibility with self-compassion and take proactive steps to reclaim your visibility. Embrace a personalized approach to health and nutrition with the support of a professional and use these tools to release the weight of invisibility. Step confidently into a more empowered, visible, and confident version of yourself.

Ann Rolle is a holistic nutrition practitioner who helps busy professional women to lose weight without dieting. She has a PhD in Holistic Nutrition and is passionate about helping women cultivate healthy satisfying relationships with their food, their bodies, and their environment so they achieve transformative results beyond just weight loss.

facebook.com/ann.b.rolle

THE SECRET SAUCE FOR MODERN CEOS: COMBINING POST-SOVIET GRIT WITH MICHELIN-STAR PRECISION FOR BUSINESS EXCELLENCE

NATALIE RUNOFF

What do post-Soviet entrepreneurship and Michelin-star cuisine have in common? At first glance, the connection might seem tenuous. After all, one speaks to the gritty, unpredictable world of economic transition and the other to the refined art of culinary excellence. Yet both share a crucial ingredient: the ability to turn adversity into advantage.

In the chaotic aftermath of the Soviet Union's collapse, newly emerged businesses faced a landscape as tumultuous as a spring thaw in the Arctic. It was a time of high inflation, economic, and political upheaval. There was a mass mosaic of people from many nations seeking to embrace their diversity after years of uniformity. Companies had to navigate these rough waters while grappling with low morale and outdated leadership models. It was a period of immense challenge but also one of enormous opportunity. In that environment, businesses needed to adapt rapidly or risk failure.

Similarly, Michelin-starred chefs operate in a world where precision and excellence are paramount. Their kitchens are not just workplaces but meticulously orchestrated environments where every detail counts. These chefs understand that true culinary artistry requires more than a high degree of technical skill; it demands a harmonious blend of creativity, teamwork, and relentless pursuit of perfection.

A Blast from the Past

Our own company was one of those fresh blooms in the post-Soviet world. In the face of obstacles, we realized something crucial: To thrive, we needed to abandon old ways and adopt a radically different approach. Our approach was straightforward yet revolutionary—connecting a human-centered approach with business objectives by:

- Embracing personal diversity as an asset
- Training middle management to empower their teams
- Fostering a culture of contribution and recognition

By continuously integrating these elements into our business operations, we have survived and risen to the top of our market niche, and we continue to maintain that position.

Fast-forward to today, and many businesses in North America are navigating similar challenges of inflation, a diverse workforce, and profitability. The good news? The lessons learned from post-Soviet business environments and insights from Michelin-starred restaurants offer a potent recipe for success that's more relevant than ever.

The Secret Sauce Ingredients

1. Embracing Diversity as an Asset

In the early days of our post-Soviet business journey, we realized that our diverse workforce was not a problem to be removed or minimized but an asset to be leveraged. The myriad cultures, languages, and viewpoints brought a richness that could fuel innovation and creativity. However, that diversity needed to be embraced and integrated into the fabric of our organization.

Like a Michelin-starred chef who blends diverse ingredients to create a culinary masterpiece, businesses must blend diverse perspectives to drive innovation. This approach requires an inclusive mindset, where every voice and every contribution is valued. Studies by McKinsey show that diverse teams are 35 percent more likely to outperform their less diverse

THE SECRET SAUCE FOR MODERN CEOS

counterparts. This isn't just about numbers; it's about harnessing the full spectrum of human experience to drive results.

2. Empowering Middle Management

Amid the post-Soviet chaos, we discovered that middle management was the linchpin of success. These managers were not just task executors but crucial connectors between the C-suite leadership focusing on delivering results to stakeholders and the frontline workers. They understood the unique challenges of their teams and could translate strategic objectives into actionable plans.

Much like the sous-chefs and line cooks in a Michelin-starred restaurant who ensure that every dish meets the highest standards, middle managers ensure that strategic goals are precisely met. Empowering these managers means equipping them with the skills and authority to make decisions, solve problems, and drive performance. It's about creating a culture where middle managers are not just enforcers but leaders who inspire and support their teams.

3. Fostering a Culture of Collaboration and Recognition

Our experience taught us that collaboration and recognition are not just buzzwords but essential ingredients for success. In the post-Soviet business landscape, we learned that creating a collaborative environment where employees are inspired and recognized leads to higher morale and better performance.

Current data supports this. According to a Gallup study, uninspired or daydreaming workers may cost businesses as much as $550 billion annually. Conversely, a *Forbes* article notes that companies that consistently motivate their employees experience a 27 percent increase in profit, a 50 percent increase in sales, a 38% increase in productivity, and a 50 percent increase in client loyalty. (Forbes article).

Michelin-starred restaurants are renowned for their meticulous attention to detail and teamwork. Every kitchen staff member, from the executive chef to the dishwasher, plays a vital role in delivering a flawless dining experience. Similarly, in a business setting, fostering a culture of collaboration and recognition ensures that every employee feels valued and motivated. This approach not only improves morale but also drives productivity and loyalty.

Connecting Soft Skills with Business Objectives: The Modern Approach

Successful businesses such as Netflix, Toyota, and Microsoft understand that soft skills are not separate from business goals; they are integral to achieving them.

Effective communication isn't just about avoiding misunderstandings; it's about aligning team efforts with strategic goals. Empathy isn't just about being nice; it's about understanding employee needs and motivations to drive performance. Teaching employees to optimize their lives is not about overreaching; it ensures higher engagement and productivity. By linking soft skills with hard business objectives, companies can create a more cohesive and motivated workforce, leading to better results.

Building a High-Performance Ecosystem

A high-performance ecosystem is one where every element, from leadership to team dynamics, works harmoniously toward common goals. This ecosystem is built on diversity, collaboration, and recognition principles. It's about creating an environment where every employee is empowered to contribute their best, and their contributions align with the company's strategic objectives.

Much like a Michelin-starred restaurant where every element, from the ingredients to the service, is meticulously crafted to deliver an exceptional dining experience, a high-performance business ecosystem requires careful cultivation. It involves investing in leadership development, fostering a culture of feedback and growth, and ensuring every employee understands their role in achieving the company's goals.

The ROI of Soft Skills: Why It Matters

Investing in soft skills isn't just a nice-to-have; it's a strategic imperative. The research underscores the importance of employee engagement in driving business success. According to recent Gallup surveys, 87 percent of workers want their employers to support their work-life balance.

THE SECRET SAUCE FOR MODERN CEOS

Engaged employees are more productive and more likely to stay with their employer. Highly engaged teams can boost company profitability by 21 percent, reduce absenteeism by 41 percent, and increase productivity by 17 percent.

These statistics highlight the practical benefits of investing in soft skills and creating a supportive work environment. Employees who feel valued and engaged are likelier to contribute their best efforts toward achieving business objectives. This, in turn, leads to better performance, higher profitability, and a more resilient organization.

The common thread between post-Soviet business resilience and Michelin-star precision lies in the strategic use of soft skills to drive hard results. In the fast-paced, often unpredictable business environment, soft skills—such as teamwork, problem-solving, and effective communication—become essential for achieving tangible success.

Traditional leadership models focused on command-and-control directives are insufficient for navigating a modern business's complexities. Instead, empowering middle managers to act as connectors between different levels of the organization is crucial. These managers translate strategic goals into actionable tasks, fostering a culture where diverse perspectives thrive.

In a similar way, Michelin-starred chefs understand the importance of teamwork and communication in their kitchens. A successful restaurant is not just about individual talent; it's about how well the team collaborates to deliver an exceptional dining experience. This level of precision and coordination is achieved through a strong emphasis on soft skills, such as active listening, constructive feedback, and fostering a positive work environment.

Facilitating Change

As a modern CEO, you can harness those lessons as an opportunity to elevate your business.

However, understanding the opportunity is one thing; implementing it effectively is another. It requires assessing your current approach to leadership and management:

- Are you empowering your middle managers to be effective connectors within your organization?

- Are you fostering a culture where soft skills are recognized, developed, and driving hard results?

Creating a system that aligns your business objectives with a focus on employee engagement, trains middle managers and employees, and builds a collaborative work environment takes time and energy, which modern CEOs often do not have.

That's why I created B.L.E.N.D., a system that empowers today's CEOs to transform soft skills into tangible outcomes, and BuzzCodex, a company that strategically packaged this potent recipe, clients' business objectives, and online learning curriculum for all staff members to facilitate long-term growth

Embrace the opportunity and watch as your business transforms into a high-performance ecosystem, ready to tackle today's challenges and seize tomorrow's opportunities.

Natalie Runoff is the founder of BuzzCodex. Drawing on her background in business, finance, and human resources, as well as multiple entrepreneurial experiences across Europe and North America, she developed B.L.E.N.D., an optimization system that enables mid-sized organizations to create high-performance ecosystems, driving hard results through soft skills.

buzzcodex.com

$AVVY STYLE: YOUR SHORTCUT TO SUCCESS

ARLENE STEARNS

"You can have anything in life you want if you dress for it!" That's not just a catchy phrase—it's wisdom from Edith Head, who won eight Academy Awards. So, imagine what you want in your life, both personally and professionally, and ask yourself: "Does my style reflect that vision?"

This applies to business too. I met Sue at a Chamber of Commerce meeting and was surprised to learn that she owned a marketing firm. I would have mistaken her for a delivery person. Like many of us, she concentrated on her business, not on the way she looked. Once we worked together and aligned her presence with her CEO status, her business skyrocketed!

Your professional presence is more powerful than you might think. The way you present yourself can either draw people in or push them away. A poor image might be costing you big time, especially when it comes to missed career opportunities. Your appearance sends a message long before you even say a word, and that message impacts everything—particularly your money and career.

Think back to the pandemic. Many of us got a little too comfortable in sweatpants and let our grooming slide. It's no wonder that some professionals found themselves sidelined, missing out on important meetings and being overlooked for promotions. If you're not putting your best foot forward—even on a video call—you might be sending the wrong message, thus costing you business, opportunities, and ultimately money.

Your career often dictates your life and income. Hiring managers rank qualifications like this:

1. Experience
2. Confidence
3. Appearance
4. Education

Yes, appearance matters that much. Before an interview, candidates are often advised to spend as much time on their appearance as on their resume. Why? Because confidence and appearance are intertwined—when you look your best, you feel your best. Those with a polished, professional appearance are more likely to get hired, advance faster, and earn more. As Deion Sanders puts it, "When you look good, you feel good, when you feel good, you play good, and when you play good, they pay good."

Maybe you're thinking, *I'm an entrepreneur (business owner, speaker)— this doesn't apply to me.* But think again. First impressions are formed in less than a second. The moment you walk into a room or step onto a stage, people decide if you're the expert they want to work with. You never get a second chance to make a first impression.

When you present a polished, professional image, people see you as more capable and credible. This boosts your chances for raises, promotions, and attracting ideal clients. Plus, when you feel good about how you look, you're more productive and appealing to others.

So, why do we resist creating a powerful personal style?

Many think it's frivolous, unaffordable, and really won't make a difference. Some think they can do it themselves and shop their way to success by purchasing more clothes that don't showcase their expertise. Those were probably my thoughts until I experienced a makeover that was the best gift ever from my mom.

In my mid-twenties, I finally got the courage to end my five-year emotionally abusive marriage. I was a total mess, my life was in shambles, and my future looked bleak! I would now become a single mom in a small town without any family nearby. Would I have the resources and support to create a new life for myself and my child?

My mom, who was a fashion model in the mid-1940s, hated seeing me so devasted, so she arranged for a makeover at Saks Fifth Avenue to uplift my spirits.

At the appointment, I felt a knot in the pit of my stomach as I watched my long, dark hair fall on the floor. After all, my hairstyle had remained the same all through high school and college. Would I regret giving permission to this stylist to create a chic look for me? Next, I was taught makeup techniques that enhanced my features. When I looked in the mirror, I barely recognized my own reflection—the results were amazing! I had been transformed from a young girl to a young professional woman! My transformation was so huge that my mother did not even recognize me! For the first time ever, I felt like a million dollars.

That's the feeling I want my clients to experience!

When I returned to my small town, the changes continued with a shopping trip to select outfits that suited the new me, but the biggest changes happened within me. My confidence soared, and I realized I could handle the challenges and create a better life.

This experience was life-changing in so many ways. It planted the seed for my future career as an image consultant and demonstrated that enhancing your appearance is a shortcut to success. After all, you are the billboard for your business!

Many of us are relearning how to dress for social and business events. Maybe you're trying on clothes that used to fit perfectly, but now . . . not so much. It's easy to blame the dryer for shrinking your clothes, but the reality is that both our bodies and styles change. Women might reach for Spanx, only to feel like a stuffed sausage that can barely breathe. And let's face it, lying down to zip up your jeans just isn't working anymore. Styles have shifted, too—those slim jeans are on their way out, and flair styles are in. Some people complain that it takes too long to look their best. But when you've mastered your personal style, getting ready becomes quick, easy, and mistake-free.

Here are some key things to consider when crafting your personal style:

1. **Focus:** Do your outfits highlight your best features? Always draw attention to your face by wearing makeup, accessories, and a V or

scoop neckline. Remember to smile; it's the best curve on your body!

2. **Fit:** Does the garment fit you—not too tight, not too loose, but just right? Does it match your personality, lifestyle, and business brand?

3. **Flatter:** Is it the right style for your body type? Check where it hits your body—avoid horizontal lines at your widest parts. Does the color work for you? Colors send subconscious messages—like blue for trustworthiness. Before you leave the house, make sure your look is on point because you're representing your brand everywhere you go.

4. **Fun:** Accessories are where you can have fun. They make the difference that helps you stand out!

When you've mastered your personal style, you'll look and feel like a leader in your industry, and people will want to work with you before you even say a word. Your polished appearance boosts your visibility and confidence in any setting, whether it's at work, social gatherings, or business functions. When your ideas are taken seriously, you're more likely to receive raises, promotions, and speaking opportunities. Entrepreneurs and business owners who embrace their unique style are seen as leaders and get paid accordingly.

When you invest in yourself, you not only improve your professional life but also your personal one. A positive self-image leads to a healthier lifestyle, stronger self-esteem, and better relationships. Your polished appearance naturally attracts others because you exude confidence and expertise.

In conclusion, your appearance affects every aspect of your life. Investing in a polished, distinctive personal style pays off in spades. Even if you're not sure where to start, know that your appearance can be transformed with the right hairstyle, makeup, and clothing that fits and flatters your body. Image consultants are experts in helping you create a style that allows you to prosper and thrive. Once you've mastered your style, you'll look like the amazing leader you are—and reap the rewards that come with it!

Style authority **Arlene Stearns**, creator of the ImageUp System, helps successful professionals to level up their image, prestige, and profits to look like a leader, so they are paid like a leader. With almost twenty years in the fashion industry, Arlene understands the powerful connection between how you look and your success.

imageupsystem.com

MESSAGING IS YOUR MARKETING—CLAIM YOUR AUTHENTIC SELF FOR BETTER CLIENTS

Kimberly Weitkamp

"Job opportunity, not spam." That was the email subject line that popped up in my inbox while I was scrolling through my email late at night in my shared apartment in Spain.

Nowadays, that phrase means "delete!" . . . but this email was from my mother. That message started me on my journey to becoming a marketing strategist and coach.

I call it my very first marketing lesson. From the first moment I saw the message, it stood out and transformed my life. That email led me to discover the world of direct response copywriting and from there the coaching and entrepreneurial world.

When I first started my business, I wrote copy. These are the words you read from a company that inspire you to take action. It can be anything from a social media post to an email to a text message and anything in between.

In the beginning, I wanted to be a behind-the-scenes-type gal. I didn't want my face in front of everybody. I didn't want to have to stand up and shout from the rooftops. I had zero interest in building a social media following.

I certainly did NOT want to be visible.

A conversation with my aunt changed my mindset. She'd been an entrepreneur for decades at that time—well before social media and the internet. And she'd built quite a recognizable brand.

On a hot and humid Florida day during a family visit, she pointed out to me how much easier the internet and social made it to build a business. But . . . I'd have to show my face. I couldn't hide on the sidelines and hope to get recognized or build a reputation.

She made it clear that visibility is key when building a business and brand online.

In fact, it's now more important than ever for us to be seen as we truly are. These days, there's a bunch of stuff out there being done by AI.

The AI overlords need reams of content to even attempt to "sound" like you, which means you being seen as yourself is the best thing you can do for yourself as a business owner.

You—your unique self—are the most saleable piece of your business. The reason somebody chooses to work with YOU instead of someone else is because they like who *you* are.

In order for you to show up and attract the right people at the right time with the right messaging, it all starts with the right mentality: "How do I get seen?"

The key piece is putting the right message in front of the right person. In order to do that, you have to be where your people are hanging out. While it's tempting to try and automate everything or hand everything off, I believe the future of business growth will be based on YOU.

My focus is on helping coaches use marketing to make money and do so in a way that aligns with who they are. I help them craft messaging that resonates with their values and goals *and* bring in the right people they LOVE working with.

We start with what I like to call your three personal items. Note: This doesn't mean needing to stuff absolutely everything you might need for a ten-day trip into a small bag you can stuff in the overhead on the plane. Instead, it's three things you're passionate about that make up who you are. To determine what these three things might be, you can ask yourself, "What do I love to do? What am I happy to talk about with strangers?"

These personal items make up some of your most visible content. This is the content people will remember.

MESSAGING IS YOUR MARKETING

We're moving out of the information age. Information used to be gated; now, it's easy to find. In the age of AI, even more content is being generated that's strictly information. Simply ask your friendly robot friend Alexa, Siri, or Google and you'll get an answer—or just put your query into a search engine.

Growing an online presence requires content that goes beyond information; it's content that stops people in their tracks and leads them to binge on everything you've created.

The reason people sit down and binge-watch hours of YouTube videos or stream on TikTok or scroll for on Facebook is that the content they are viewing is unique.

It stands out.

Often the memorable content that brings people in isn't factual—it's the stories you tell and those personal items you talk about. It could be anything from your love of hiking or your deep hatred of sushi or your obsession with every *Star Wars* film ever made.

These personal items are what makes us stand out, be relatable, be remembered, and build our visibility profile. Keep in mind:

- Online visibility is a part of marketing.
- Marketing is your messaging.
- Messaging is your marketing.
- Marketing is your business.
- Without marketing, you can't grow a business.

Field of Dreams makes a good point—but I take it a step further and say that if you build it, they will NOT come unless you tell them about it.

Unless you show up and share about you, your business, the people you serve, and the problems you solve, no one will know your business exists.

When was the last time you had a problem with something you bought? Whether it was a TV subscription, a cell phone, or something you wanted to return to Amazon, you probably went through fifteen different hoops trying to get a real freaking person on the phone.

Your problem might eventually have gotten solved. But after you were routed through sixteen automated menus and had pressed "0" a dozen times, you probably thought to yourself, *If I could only talk to a real person!*

More and more content is available every day online. A lot of it isn't great. Even more of it is horrible.

When you incorporate marketing that lets you stand out as your true, authentic self, you are the person people will want to work with, and you will stand out above the noise.

In today's environment, people will tell you to do a lot of things to utilize a marketing strategy—everything from go live on TikTok or Facebook every day to email your list daily. These are tactics—and they aren't your strategy.

Instead, focus on what matters, where your people are, and where you need to be seen, and then tailor your messaging so you attract the people you want to work with and can get the best results for. Don't worry about anybody else.

If you need permission to stop pleasing everybody, you now have it. I grant it to you.

When you try and please everyone, you end up pleasing no one. So the next time it's time for you to get out in front, be seen, and be heard in your marketing strategy, don't worry about being everything to everyone. Instead, take the time know where you want to talk, to stand out and be your true, authentic self. There is no right or wrong when it comes to messaging. There's only messaging that resonates and messaging that repels. You want your ideal audience and your ideal clients to see the messaging that resonates with them. Who cares about anybody else?

I'll leave you with a short story. When I was a child, I would go to school with mismatched socks. It wasn't a mistake. It was actually purposeful, and I continued to do it for years. It was part of my personality. It was part of how I showed up. It was unique, it was quirky, and it made me memorable.

I wasn't trying to seek attention. Instead, I would ask myself every morning, "What pattern do I want to explore today?"

But soon enough, my teachers took my uniqueness and tried to stuff it in a box. They told me, "Be quiet," when I would answer too many questions. They went to my parents and asked if there was something wrong at home because clearly my parents couldn't dress me properly.

My mother could have told me, "You need to stop mixing your socks." Instead, she told my teachers, "This is the way she likes to express herself."

You see, there is no right way to be you. The only right way to be you is to *be you*. The same is true in marketing, especially when building your personal brand, coaching, or service professional business.

How can you be the best version of you online? Start as you mean to go on. Don't censor. And don't worry about others' feelings.

Just be you.

Kimberly Weitkamp is known as the Audience Converter. With more than ten years of experience, she works with coaches to craft marketing that makes money *and* aligns with their values, goals, and calendar. She's host of the Top 3 Percent Globally Ranked *More Conversations, Clients & Cash* podcast.

theaudienceconverter.com

THE COMEBACK—RECLAIMING YOUR SASSY SPIRIT

SHAYE WOODWARD

I'm sitting in the car all by myself, screaming at the top of my lungs. I am so angry. I needed to get away from him. I've heard it again for the millionth time: "It's your issue, not mine—when are you going to fix yourself? You're the problem, not me. When are you going to stop being so neurotic, so over the top, so much?"

I had tried over and over again so many times to get in control, get in order, fix myself, fix my world . . . and NOTHING seemed to work.

This was just one more time when I would review everything in my life, point out to myself all the mistakes, all the failures, all that I did wrong or wasn't good enough to get the results or meet the deadlines and expectations of myself and others.

What's the point to all of this? If I can't measure up, then what am I doing? Why do I keep hitting these brick walls?

I was in my mid-thirties. I felt so broken inside and felt like that's all I would be for the rest of my life—broken and never good enough.

I was so tired. I was staying up until one or two o'clock in the morning, making sure the house was in order, dishes done, laundry folded, toys put away before going to bed and finally collapsing to get some sleep.

That is, until my husband got upset that I didn't go to bed when he went to bed. Another time that I was not doing the right things, not being a good enough wife or mom.

I changed it again and slept when he wanted, did chores when he wanted. It got to the point when I didn't think I could make the right decisions anymore. This was not living; this was existing, doing what everyone else was telling me to do and doing it their way. This was not what I thought it was going to be like as an adult.

The years passed, and now I was in my forties, still feeling like I had made such a mess of my life. Here I was, divorced twice and on my third marriage, which was about to implode also. I had just found out my husband was using drugs.

I felt like a loser, and even worse, I felt like I had ruined my kids' lives with all the choices I had made. I had become a burden, of no value to anyone. I had to ask my oldest son for help to get out of this situation and keep my younger two boys, his brothers, safe. He agreed to help us, and we moved into an apartment together, hoping to start fresh, move forward, and heal.

This changed the trajectory of my life. For the first time, I took a stand for myself. Enough was enough, and I decided I did not have to live like this. For perhaps the first time, I saw that I had value and worth inside of me that I had never tapped into before.

It was the beginning of a new life, a new world, a new me.

I had been embarrassed by what society considered to be a failure that I became the failure inside of me. I couldn't seem to figure out the "right" way to live and be a success. I kept thinking, *What more do I need to do to prove that I'm good enough? What am I doing that has caused me to live such a chaotic, overwhelming, and highly anxious life?*

And then it hit me!

What was wrong with me was that I'd been looking at my entire life and constantly focusing on what was wrong with me. But now I was seeking to find out what was *right* with me. I started asking some different questions:

- Who am I?
- What do I want to be in this life?
- How can I be who I am meant to be?

Still, I was a mom of five children, had been married three times and was divorcing my third husband. When it came to relationships, who would want to be with me?

I concluded that I wasn't good enough to be married, to have a companion I could trust, to find love or a partner for life.

THE COMEBACK—RECLAIMING YOUR SASSY SPIRIT

Then something happened.

While getting our certification in a relationships class, my friend and I were talking with our mentor. She asked both of us to co-teach the class. Honestly, I wasn't quite sure why she wanted me to teach a relationships class. Didn't she already see I had three failed marriages?

But as we started preparing, we became really close friends. I realized that I was not broken inside; there was nothing wrong with me—just something wrong with my "chooser." I had a broken chooser.

This friendship grew into a relationship. Now both of us are in our fourth marriage—together— and it's one of the happiest and most content marriages either of us have had. We love each other, even in the ups and downs.

But that's not the best part. The best part is being able to find myself. I do not mean this in a cliché way. I had been searching for so long to find her, and my entire adult life I had felt that I didn't really have a voice. I was not allowed to be me. I had to fit into the crowd, be like everyone else, not stand out, not be myself.

It's a funny story how I finally found her. It all happened in the matter of a couple of seconds. You see, I had a ding on my phone—a text message from my dad. Apprehensively I opened the text—I was never sure what would come from him—and I instantly started to cry. In that text message was a picture: a picture of me when I was about six years old.

It was her!

I found her!

She had been gone for so long.

There she was with her hands on her hips, a smile on her face with a sassy look, just exuding confidence.

At that moment I realized that I was okay, and I would be okay from now on. I finally know who I am. I am a kind, loving daughter of God with light and value for others.

Now I'm free to be me again. I no longer feel like I'm different and that's a problem. And whenever I begin to think, *I'm not good enough, I'm not fitting in, I'm broken*, I just look at her and know those are all just lies.

It's okay for me to be me, learning how to use my brain, learning how to make things work the way I need them, and teach others the way it works for their brains.

Why is this important to me? Well, if I am a person with light and value for others, then I need to be visible enough to allow others to find their way too. They do not have to struggle with all that garbage, and wait for years, or even decades, to find themselves

All the years of pain, of feeling like I'm not worthy, of no value, or not good enough have led me here, where I am able to bless someone else to be able to have a great life too.

What about you? How can you become visible to lead the others to where you are and allow them to have the joy in life that they deserve?

It's time to step out of the shadows of shame and blame. It's time to step into the light and show others what is possible. You know how to help them because you were there, and now you are here.

As it says in Matthew 5:16 (KJV), "Let your light so shine before men that they may see your good works…"

It's time to be visible; it's time to let your light shine. In this way, those who are praying for an answer, or for direction, or for their next step may see your light, and you will be able to help them step forward and shine their own light and be visible to those who need them.

So pull out your candle, pull out your flashlight, pull out your phone, turn on those lights, and lead the way!

Shaye Woodward is a relationship specialist and master certified coach dedicated to assisting couples and individuals navigating the unique challenges associated with ADHD. She has become an advocate for transforming ADHD struggles into strength. She and her husband are co-authors of the book *Winning the Human Race*.

winningthehumanrace.com/adhd-style

Milton Keynes UK
Ingram Content Group UK Ltd.
UKHW032049231124
451423UK00013B/1202